The Writing Experience

Carol Schoen
Elaine Avidon
Nila Gandhi
James Vaughn

Lehman College

Canadian Edition published 1981 by McClelland and Stewart
Reprinted 1991

ISBN 0-7710-8002-6
McClelland & Stewart Inc., *The Canadian Publishers*
481 University Avenue, Toronto   M5G 2E9
Printed and bound in Canada

ACKNOWLEDGMENTS

The authors gratefully acknowledge permission to use material from the following sources:

Text

One   Pages 8–9 From "First Love" in *Stand Still like the Hummingbird* by Henry Miller. Copyright © 1962 by Henry Miller. Reprinted by permission of New Directions Publishing Corporation.
Page 9 From Doris Lessing, *Martha Quest*. Copyright © 1952, 1954, 1964 by Doris Lessing. Reprinted by permission of Simon & Schuster, a Division of Gulf & Western Corporation.

Two   Page 16 Lines from "The Love Song of J. Alfred Prufrock" from *Collected Poems 1909–1962* by T. S. Eliot reprinted by permission of Harcourt Brace Jovanovich, Inc., and Faber and Faber Ltd.
Page 16 Lines from "Harlem," copyright 1951 by Langston Hughes. Reprinted from *The Panther and the Lash*, by Langston Hughes, by permission of Alfred A. Knopf, Inc.
Page 17 Lines from "Mother to Son," copyright 1926 by Alfred A. Knopf, Inc. and renewed 1954 by Langston Hughes. Reprinted from *Selected Poems of Langston Hughes* by permission of Alfred A. Knopf, Inc.
Pages 20–21 Excerpts abridged from pp. 190–192 of *Zen and the Art of Motorcycle Maintenance* by Robert M. Pirsig. Copyright © 1974 by Robert M. Pirsig. By permission of William Morrow & Company.

Three   Pages 34–42 "A Worn Path," copyright 1941, 1969 by Eudora Welty. Reprinted from her volume *A Curtin of Green and Other Stories* by permission of Harcourt Brace Jovanovich, Inc.

Four   Pages 48–49 Russell Baker, "School vs. Education," *The New York Times*, September 1977. © 1977 by The New York Times Company. Reprinted by permission.
Page 51 Characteristics of an Instructor from *Nothing Never Happens* by Kenneth G. Johnson, John J. Senatore, Mark C. Liebig, and Gene Minor. Copyright © 1974 by Benziger Bruce & Glencoe Co., Inc. Reprinted by permission of Macmillan Publishing Co., Inc.
Pages 52–53 From "How 'Bigger' Was Born" by Richard Wright, *The Saturday Review of Literature*, 1 June 1940. By permission.
Page 53 "Adolf Hitler," from *Caesars in Goosestep* by W. D. Bayles, p. 45, Harper Bros., New York, 1940.
Pages 55–56 From *Down These Mean Streets* by Piri Thomas, pp. 70–71. Copyright © 1967 by Piri Thomas. Reprinted by permission of Alfred A. Knopf, Inc.

Five   Page 67 Adapted from *A Death in the Family* by James Agee. Copyright © 1957 by The James Agee Trust. Used by permission of Grosset & Dunlap, Inc.
Pages 68–70 "Pangee Trap" from *Rumor of War* by Philip Caputo. Copyright © 1977 by Philip Caputo. Reprinted by permission of Holt, Rinehart and Winston, Inc.

(Acknowledgments continued on page 236).

Preface

A developmental composition text must present more than a one-dimensional approach. The wide swings in attitude that have marked the past two decades have caused developmental composition teachers to reassess their premises and techniques in the light of their own experiences. In planning for this text, we examined the open, permissive approach of the 1960s and the "return to the basics" of the 1970s and accepted those parts of each that we consider necessary and valuable. Our aim has been to produce a text that integrates carefully structured basic skills components with purposeful and challenging classroom and writing experiences, and at the same time maintains enough flexibility to allow individual teachers to adapt the text to meet their students' needs.

In meeting this goal, our first task was to formulate a suitable definition of the students in developmental composition classes. During the 1960s such students were described as having "academically squashed ego [s]" [1] (Kressey, 1971), and texts were written to make students feel good about themselves. More recent definitions have included such assessments as "paucity . . . of vocabu-

[1] Michael Kressey, "The Community College Student: A Lesson in Humility," *College English*, 32 (April 1971) 772.

lary, lack of syntactic maturity . . ." [2] (Lunsford, 1978), and developmental composition texts of the 1970s have emphasized strengthening the students' basic skills. But it is our contention that students do not write well because they lack both the skills and the confidence to do so. A successful developmental composition text should, therefore, consider the interrelationship of both these factors.

The primary goal of *The Writing Experience* is to help high school students cope with the presentation of their ideas clearly and precisely in acceptable written English. To accomplish this goal, we have provided a text that focuses on the total situation. Grammar, rhetoric, and precision and clarity of detail are identifiably separate items for a teacher; but for a writer, especially a beginning writer, they are all part of the same process. To cope with this fact, we have combined the elements that fit together naturally.

In Part 1, Description, where vivid language is of primary importance, we have concentrated on word choice, use of modifiers, and their integration into the sentence. Rhetorical organization is presented in its simplest form, so that students can concentrate on description. In Part 2, Narration, where action assumes greater importance, verb structures and forms fit most naturally. Compound and complex sentence structures are part of the more complex thought involved in argument; thus they are placed in Part 3, Exposition. But regardless of the rhetorical or syntactic focus, students are always asked to write complete essays and, in each essay, to make use of what they have learned in the previous chapters.

Students do not have only cognitive problems with their writing. Generally, they view themselves as poor at expressing their thoughts in writing, since that is how they have been judged. The impact of this history, a subject-related affect, is described by Benjamin Bloom (1978):

> If his performance has been inadequate, the student comes to believe in his inadequacy with respect to this type of learning. He approaches the next tasks in the series with marked reluctance. He expects the worst. If it is painful enough, the task is avoided, or at least approached with little enthusiasm or marked dislike. Where the student is convinced of his in-

[2] Andrea Lunsford, "What We Know — and Don't Know — about Remedial Writing," *College Composition and Communication*, 29 (Feb. 1978) 47.

adequacy, he finds no great energy to accomplish the next task, has little patience or perserverance when he encounters difficulties and takes little care and thoroughness in accomplishing the task.[3]

Each chapter begins with a group activity related to the subject matter of the chapter, and also designed to break down the barriers that usually make students feel isolated and uncomfortable in academic situations. The writing assignments grow out of students' own experiences, encouraging them in the belief that they, as unique individuals, have contributions to make.

Such efforts in the affective area are useless, however, unless the students actually gain mastery in specific areas of writing. To this end we have broken down the writing skills into small, easily learned segments that build on each other. Thus, matters that deal with developing students' confidence in themselves as learners and as writers are always related to the development of specific writing skills.

Finally, we have attempted to integrate the material within each chapter. In most instances, the initial activity is the basis for the in-class writing assignment that prefigures the formal essay at the end of the chapter. The activity provides the preliminary thought, while the in-class writing provides a working, prewriting experience. Students are given a chance to think through an issue, as well as to explore ways of presenting their ideas in words before the final assignment. The formal writing, however, is always the product of the individual, for all students are given the opportunity to arrive at their own conclusions.

Despite the efforts we have made to integrate the elements of the text, flexibility is maintained. There is still ample room for individual instructors to rearrange the material to suit their own teaching needs.

We have used certain terms that may need clarification:

Activity — The activities are essentially group experiences that stimulate student participation and focus on a particular topic that will be the subject of the final formal writing assignment. The time spent on any one activity can vary from a few minutes to a whole class period, to suit the individual instructor's preference.

[3] Benjamin Bloom, *Human Characteristics and School Learning* (New York: McGraw Hill, 1976), pp. 145–46.

In-Class Writing — These are focused, free-writing situations, and should be judged as such. Students should be encouraged to share their ideas, so that they can stimulate each other. In most cases, these writings treat subjects that will be handled in the formal essays also, so that, in effect, students are given the opportunity of preparing a preliminary draft. It is usually not useful to correct grammar at this point, but if teachers look at the papers they should point out problem areas.

Language Learning — These units present both grammatical and rhetorical materials. The earlier sections focus more on grammar; the later, more on rhetoric. There are some exercises in the text itself, and in the appendix there is material for extra work in grammar. The language learning units may be used earlier or later than they appear in the book.

Formal Writing — These essays are usually written at home, and they should be treated as applications of what has been presented earlier in the chapter, as well as in previous chapters. This format is designed to help students learn how to prepare a first draft and rewrite, a concept they are not generally familiar with.

In creating this text we have been fortunate to have had the help of a great many people — our students, who suffered through our efforts to refine our techniques; our colleagues in the Academic Skills Department at Lehman College: Leonard Bernstein, Sheila Hobson, Richard Sterling, Elizabeth Stone, and Loretta Taylor, who generously suggested alternate methods and ideas; and our editors at Little, Brown: Katherine Carlone, Sheryl Gipstein, Cynthia Chapin, and Jan Young, who encouraged us and kept our spirits up. We are particularly grateful to a number of people whom we have never met — those who read the manuscript and offered detailed criticism: Joseph E. Trimmer, Roberta S. Matthews, Peter Lindblom, and Richard S. Beal; but most especially to Karl K. Taylor, who in a "fatherly, precise" way guided our initial ideas into a workable, finished form. And, of course, our thanks go to our families and friends whose tolerance and support buoyed us up during the difficult times.

Contents

To the Student

When four people write a book together, they spend a lot of time talking, and not all of it has to do with the book. One afternoon the four of us recalled our earliest memories of writing. We'd like to share these with you because they emphasize the struggles so many people have as they try to break through their negative attitudes toward writing.

Nila was in Standard Four (fourth grade) in a boarding school in India. It was the monsoon season. The teacher asked each student to write an autobiography. Nila concluded that there was nothing she could write about herself that would interest her teacher, and so she lied. She invented experiences, adventures, and even family members — the perfect family in the perfect world. She made up the entire autobiography.

Jim lived in Xenia, Ohio. When he was 15, he went to see the movie *Rebecca*. He came home inspired and decided to write his own story. He carefully selected paper and pencil and then proceeded to cover the pages with doodles and drawings. When he gave up, not one word had been written.

During her senior year in Plainfield High School in New Jersey, Carol was assigned a paper on her most embarrassing experience. She felt that her entire life was one big embarrassing experience and therefore there were too many stray ends. She made up a story about a mix-up in a play where she saved the day.

Elaine was in the seventh grade at P.S. 178 in Queens, New York. Each student in the class had to write a composition about a national park. She chose the Grand Teton National Park but, never having been there nor to any other national park, she copied word for word everything the Encyclopedia Britannica had to say about the park.

Lies, plagiarism, nothing — writing is not easy. But it is possible for writing to become manageable and even pleasurable. Often when we have to do or create or make something for the first time the task seems impossible; but once we begin to understand the parts of what we are about to do, it at least seems manageable. Think about skiing. It is not a natural way of moving, but once you learn to ski it feels as natural as if you had been doing it all your life. As a beginner, just attaching boots to the bindings looks difficult, but once you understand a buckle or two the task is easily mastered. Then you learn to snow plow, to ski parallel, and to get on and off the rope tow. The next thing you know, you have gone up the chair lift and are parallel skiing and parallel turning down the trail. Though most people do not become hot doggers, they do, after they master the various aspects of the sport, become good enough to enjoy the thrill of swiftly moving down a splendid, snow covered slope.

Writing is not so different from skiing. It, too, does not feel natural in the beginning, but once you grasp the various aspects of the process, writing can feel natural as a method of expressing ideas. Essays are composed of parts, and learning to handle one part of the essay makes it more possible to learn to handle the next part. Eventually, through a thorough understanding of each part, you can comfortably and confidently write well-formulated, whole essays.

The purpose of this text is to develop your skills and strengthen your confidence in yourself as a writer of essays. Each chapter of the three divisions of the book teaches one or two small parts of essay writing. By the time this course is complete, you will fully comprehend the components of the essay and you will have numerous opportunities to practise writing essays. Every activity and assignment in this book is included because it teaches some aspect of writing. As a result of being given the opportunity to understand and master that which is being asked of you, we hope that you will be more true to yourselves than we were to ourselves in our early writing assignments.

In each chapter, you will have both an in-class and a formal writing assignment. In-class essays are your first attempts at using the particular aspect of essay writing that the chapter teaches. It is important for your development as a writer that you take risks in writing these essays. Try out your ideas and try your hand at whatever aspect of writing the assignment stresses. Don't be afraid of mistakes. No writer, not even the most famous or the most accomplished, expects perfection of a first draft or a first try at a particular form of writing. Be prepared to cross out, change, and add. Just try as hard as you can to use the skills you have been taught, and then use your experience with the particular assignment to understand those aspects of writing that still give you trouble.

Formal essays are written after you have read about, discussed, and practised the particular aspect of writing presented in the chapter. These assignments take time to plan, write, rewrite, and proofread. In fact, it is likely that they will be written three, four, or five times before you are satisfied with the results. At the end of each formal writing assignment there is a checklist. Use this list to help yourself plan and evaluate your own formal essays.

Description occurs in all writing — witches are described in fairy tales, cells in biology texts, wars in history books. A description communicates the writer's perceptions; when a writer describes the fat man gorging candy bars at the fair, the colorful headdress of an Aztec chief, or the view of Toronto by night from atop the C. N. Tower, readers should be able to see, hear, taste, smell, touch, and feel what is being described.

When you, the writer, describe people, places, or things, you help your readers to understand more clearly and completely what you are trying to tell them. In the first three chapters of this book, you will discover what a good description is and how to go about writing one yourself. The activities in Chapter 1 of this part will help you get to know your classmates. You will focus on using specific and precise words to describe people. In Chapter 2, the focus of your activities, experiences, and writing will be on describing objects. You will learn to recognize and make use of words that describe physical qualities and at the same time communicate feelings. In Chapter 3, you will acquire techniques for describing places and scenes that may include both people and things; you will also learn how to select words and phrases to make your descriptions clear, detailed, and vivid.

Chapter One

Describing a Person

The real reason for writing is to communicate with others —
"to reach out and touch" — so that you are not alone, but are part
of the human race; you belong. Now here you are, a group of
students bound together by a common purpose — to learn to
write. One way to begin is to try to open up some channels of
communication.

In this, the first chapter of this part, you will get to know one
another well enough to become at least friendly strangers. Then
each of you will describe a person in the room. Since one of the
primary requirements of effective description and in fact of all
writing is to know your subject, what better way to achieve this
goal than to have the subject of your description before you — to
look at, to talk with, to find out about. As you participate in activities, communicate with one another, read other writers' descriptions, and write your own descriptions, you will discover the importance of using *specific* and *concrete* words to make your
writing a vibrant picture in words.

ACTIVITY   **Introducing a Stranger**   One way to get to know everyone in
the class is to begin by meeting one other person in the class. Pick
a student you don't know well and talk with him or her for about
20 minutes. First, let's think about the kinds of questions you
might want to ask. Some questions will occur to almost everyone —
"What school did you come from?" "How many brothers and sisters do you have?" But are these really helpful or interesting? Do

they really aid you in getting to know the person you are talking to?

Below are some questions that may serve your purpose better:

1. Do you like cars, stereos, TV? What equipment do you own or would you like to own? Why?
2. What would you do if you had a million dollars?
3. What kind of people do you like to be with?
4. What makes you angry, sad, happy, bored?
5. What was the greatest experience you ever had? What was the worst?
6. Do you like going to discos, football games, McDonald's?
7. Do you like rock music? What group do you like best? Why?
8. Do you like going to movies by yourself? or with others? What kinds of films? Why?
9. What is your opinion of:
   a. drinking?
   b. cheating on tests?
   c. smoking?
   d. corporal punishment in school?
   e. the death penalty?
10. Have you ever had a summer job? Are you working part-time now? What kind of job or jobs have you had? Which did you enjoy? Which did you hate? Why?

See if you can think of more unusual questions that might give you an insight into the other person's character. As the members of the group suggest new questions, your teacher or a classmate can write the most interesting ones on the board.

Once the questions have been selected, find a student you don't know well and start an interview. You may ask all your questions first and then answer all the other person's, or the two of you may alternate; use any order that makes you both comfortable. If one of the questions leads you into an interesting discussion, don't hesitate to follow it up with related questions. Some of you might find it helpful to take notes during the conversation.

At the end of the time period, reassemble as a group. Introduce your partner to the class by telling some of the things you have discussed. If you think of any questions as other members of the group are being introduced, feel free to ask them.

Discussion

Now that you know a little more about one another than you did at the beginning of the lesson, let's talk about this activity.

1. During this activity, did you hesitate to ask certain questions that came to mind? What does this tell you about yourself? about the other person? About interviews you read?
2. How did it feel to introduce a person who was not well known to you until a few minutes ago?
3. Did this experience tell you anything about how students behave in a classroom?
4. Did this activity break down some of the barriers to communication? If so, how and why? If not, what ways would you suggest that might have worked better?
5. How differently do you feel now about this class from the way you did when you first walked into the room?
6. Do you think that this activity will help this class work together to learn to write well?

IN-CLASS WRITING

Writing About New People and New Situations

Keeping this experience in mind, write about (1) a past experience of meeting someone for the first time, or (2) the first day in some other class.

If you are writing about a past experience of meeting someone for the first time, for instance, at a party, you may write something like this:

> I was a little nervous in my new outfit and my first pair of high heels as I opened the door and looked at a sea of laughing, talking faces and gaily dressed people spinning around the room. Disco rock exploded in my ears like a rocket after the empty stillness of the street outside. My fears of it being another boring party disappeared as I made my way excitedly toward my friend through a maze of whirling bodies.
>
> All of a sudden, I bumped into something and felt a wet icy-cold sensation running down my left leg. I looked down and watched in dismay as a golden brown stain spread its fingers over the white satin of my skirt, while a deep, soft voice murmured endless apologies in my ear. Angry and

close to tears, I looked up straight into a pair of concerned black-brown eyes and forgot all about the dress I had spent all my savings on. "I'm extremely sorry," he said for the tenth time, "but since we can't do much about the Coke why don't we dance and let your skirt dry out?" I couldn't think of a thing to say, but we danced and danced until we were so thirsty we had to stop for a drink. As we picked up two Cokes, we looked at each other and burst into laughter. It was suddenly so easy to talk. The rest of the evening just flew by as we danced and talked and laughed together till the party was over and he walked me home. He left me at my front door with a good-night kiss on my cheek and my telephone number in his pocket.

As I got into bed, tired but happy, I thought to myself, how easy it is to become friends with a stranger, especially a gentle, humorous stranger with warm black-brown eyes and a deep soft voice.

You will have noticed that the writer's experience naturally falls into three parts — how she felt before the party, what she experienced during the party, and, finally, her thoughts and feelings after the party. The same kind of order of events might also apply if you wish to write about your recollections of a first day in a new class. You might begin by telling what your thoughts, feelings, and expectations were before you went to the class. In the next paragraph, you might describe what actually happened during the class, and then you would end by telling your impressions and feelings after the class was over.

Whichever of the two topics you decide to write about, if you start at the beginning of your experience and follow it through step by step till you come to the end, you will find it easy to write and your readers will find it easy to understand.

Finally, remember that an in-class writing is for yourself, so don't be anxious about the mistakes you might make. If you are still unclear about what an in-class writing assignment is, reread pp. 4–5.

LANGUAGE LEARNING

Avoiding Vague Words Read the following description and see if it fits anyone in your class. As you read it, consider why it is not a good description.

Read

This Person

This person is of medium height and average build. This person is good looking with a nicely shaped body and a pleasant smile. The skin is light and the complexion is O.K. ~~This person has short, dark hair and brown eyes.~~ The nose is just right for the face. The ears are not too big and not too small. The neck is long. This person has rather small hands and regular fingers. The legs are fine and the feet are normal.

This person has a nice personality. This person is a good person and is also kind and friendly. This person has good taste in clothes and likes to dress casually. This person usually wears blue jeans and a red, green, or blue top. This person's hobbies are partying and going to the movies.

In the blanks, answer the following questions:

1. Which person in the class fits this description? _____
2. How many people in the class are of:
   a. medium height? _____
   b. average build? _____
3. How many people in the class do you think:
   a. are good looking? _____
   b. have nicely shaped bodies? _____
4. How many people in the class have:
   a. pleasant smiles? _____
   b. light skins? _____
   c. O.K. complexions? _____
   d. ~~short, dark hair?~~ _____
   e. ~~brown eyes?~~ _____
5. How many people's noses are just right for their faces? _____
6. How many people's ears are not too big and not too small? _____
7. How many people have:
   a. long necks? _____
   b. rather small hands? _____
   c. regular fingers? _____
   d. fine legs? _____
   e. normal feet? _____
8. How many people have nice personalities? _____
9. How many people are:
   a. good? _____
   b. kind? _____
   c. friendly? _____

10. How many:
  a. have good taste in clothes? _____
  b. dress casually? _____
  c. wear blue jeans? _____
  d. have on red, green, or blue tops? _____
11. How many people's hobbies are:
  a. partying? _____
  b. going to the movies? _____

Discussion

You can see that the description of this person is poor because it could fit several people in the class, and that some of the items of description even apply to everyone.

1. What could you do to improve this description?
2. Pick out the vague words in the description. What do they have in common?

The main drawback of the description above is the use of words like *good, nice, pleasant,* and *regular.* These words create problems because they do not tell clearly and precisely what you mean. What made the person look good to the writer of this piece? For instance, could you tell whether this person had a marble smooth, wide forehead? sparkling, nut-brown eyes with long, thick, curled eyelashes? a slim, straight nose? dimpled cheeks? a full mouth that curves up mischievously at the corners? a strong, square jaw? Or what gave you the impression that this person had a "nice" personality? Did he or she show a real interest in you or make you laugh? Did the person's eyes light up when you said something? In other words, to write a clear and effective description — whether of physical appearance or of personality — you must choose the words that tell exactly what creates the impression you are describing.

IN-CLASS WRITING

Writing a Group Description of a Person Together with a few members of the class you are going to write a description. The following steps should help make this process easier:

1. First, with the whole class working together, list on the board the details you consider important in describing a person. List these items in three categories: face, body, and personality.

2. Now split up in groups of three or four. Working together as groups, write a description of one person in the class. The person may be a member of your group, but that is not required.
3. The description should consist of three paragraphs. Paragraph 1 should describe the face; paragraph 2, the body; and paragraph 3, the personality. Make up a name for the person that seems to fit. All should contribute ideas, but each group will produce only one paper. Therefore, you should select one member of your group to act as secretary.
4. At the end of 15 or 20 minutes, reassemble as a class so that each group may read its description. Before the descriptions are read, all members of the class should stand up. When any item of description is read that *does not* fit you, you should sit down and remain seated. If the paper is specific, there should be only one person standing at the end.

Discussion

1. In what ways did the group descriptions differ from the description called "This Person"?
2. What words did you use that helped you see the individual you described as he or she really is?

READING

As you read the following passages, see if you can tell what makes each of these selections vivid.

FIRST LOVE — Henry Miller

In my mind's eye I can see her today just as vividly as when I first met her, which was in one of the corridors of Eastern District High School (Brooklyn) as she was going from one classroom to another. She was just a little shorter than I, well built, that is to say rather buxom, radiant, bursting with health, head high, glance at once imperious and saucy, concealing a shyness which was disconcerting. She had a warm, generous mouth filled with rather large, dazzling white teeth. But it was her hair and eyes which drew one first. Light golden hair it was, combed up stiff in the form of a conch. A natural blonde such as one seldom sees except in an opera. Her eyes, which were extremely limpid, were full and round. They were a China blue, and they matched her golden hair and her apple-blossom complexion. She was only sixteen, of course, and not very sure of herself, though she seemed to give the impression that she was. She stood out from all the other girls in the school, like someone with blue blood in her veins. Blue blood and icy, I am tempted to say.

MARTHA QUEST — Doris Lessing

Mr. Jasper Cohen already owned her heart because of a quality one might imagine would make it impossible: he was hideously ugly. No, not hideously: he was fantastically ugly, so ugly the word hardly applied. He was short, he was squat, he was pale; but these were words one might as justly use for Joss, his nephew, or for his brother, Max. His body was broad beyond squareness; it had a swelling, humped look. His head was enormous; a vast, pale, domed forehead reached to a peak where the hair began, covering a white, damp scalp in faint oily streaks, and breaking above the ears into a black fuzz that seemed to Martha pathetic, like the tender, defenceless fuzz of a baby's head. His face was inordinately broad, a pale, lumpy expanse, with a flat, lumpy nose, wide, mauvish lips, and ears rioting out on either side like scrolls. His hands were equally extraordinary: broad, deep palms puffed themselves into rolls of thick white flesh, ending in short, spatulate fingers almost as broad as long. They were the hands of a grotesque; and as they moved clumsily in a drawer, looking for something, Martha watched them in suspense, wishing she might offer to help him. She longed to do something for him; for this ugly man had something so tender and sweet in his face, together with the stubborn dignity of an afflicted person who intends to make no apologies or claims for something he cannot help, that she was asking herself, What is ugliness? She was asking it indignantly, the protest directed against nature itself; and, perhaps for the first time in her life she wondered with secret gratitude what it would be like to be born plain, born ugly, instead of into, if not the aristocracy, at least the middle classes of good looks.

Discussion

1. What made these passages more vivid than "This Person"?
2. In both passages, what is the order in which physical appearance is described?

3. Is there a pattern in each writer's description? For example, does Henry Miller describe her from head to toe, or does he move from the whole to the particular, or from the least striking to the most striking features?
4. Identify the adjectives that the writers use to describe the various features. What general impression do they convey to you of the appearance of the girl and the man described?
5. Can you group each of these adjectives into more than one category? If so, do the categories modify the general impression?

<table>
<tr><td>LANGUAGE
LEARNING</td><td>

Word Meaning If you were walking down a street, you would have no trouble recognizing the schoolboy's "first love" or Mr. Cohen because the writers, Henry Miller and Doris Lessing, described the striking characteristics in the appearance of both the characters in vivid words. For instance, when Miller describes the girl's body, he uses the word *buxom,* and when Lessing depicts Mr. Cohen's fingers, she calls them *lumpy.* The dictionary defines *buxom* as *plump* and *lumpy* as *fat.* However, the phrases, *a plump body* or *fat fingers* do not arouse sensory and emotional responses. They provide the literal scene, but not the emotional flavor.

</td></tr>
</table>

Word Meaning If you were walking down a street, you would have no trouble recognizing the schoolboy's "first love" or Mr. Cohen because the writers, Henry Miller and Doris Lessing, described the striking characteristics in the appearance of both the characters in vivid words. For instance, when Miller describes the girl's body, he uses the word *buxom,* and when Lessing depicts Mr. Cohen's fingers, she calls them *lumpy.* The dictionary defines *buxom* as *plump* and *lumpy* as *fat.* However, the phrases, *a plump body* or *fat fingers* do not arouse sensory and emotional responses. They provide the literal scene, but not the emotional flavor.

The literal meaning of words is called *denotative.* It names or identifies an object, but it does not elicit a sensory image or an emotional response. In vivid writing, the good writer tries to evoke strong feelings in the reader. To achieve this purpose, a writer looks for words that excite, shock, or in some way stir up the audience. The ability of words to arouse this kind of response is called *connotative.*

Below are several denotative words frequently used to describe people. Next to each is a series of more vivid, connotative words. As you read through them, you will notice that some of them arouse pleasant images, while others are distinctly unpleasant. Try to decide which ones you would use for someone you like and which you would use for someone you dislike.

fat   chubby, buxom, overweight, robust, heavy, stout, corpulent, obese, thick, plump

thin   slim, slender, willowy, spindly, scrawny, wizened, lean, emaciated, wispy

smooth   silky, glassy, velvety, sleek, glazed, satiny

short	stumpy, tiny, squat, dwarfish, puny, petite, little, stunted, runty, diminutive
tall	lanky, rangy, towering, gangling, stringy, statuesque
colorless	pallid, ashen, pasty, white, anemic, pale

Write two short paragraphs, each describing a person with some of the characteristics named in the column on the left. One description should create a pleasant impression and the other, an unpleasant one.

FORMAL WRITING

Describing Someone You Know Well   Through the interviews with your classmates, all of you have become acquainted with one another and you have worked to establish a more relaxed community. You have learned that it is important to know the subject of your description. Finally, you have learned the necessity of choosing the specific and precise words to convey your perceptions. Now you will use what you have learned in your first formal writing.

Think of a person you know really well — a member of your family, a neighbor, a close friend. Plan to be with that person for an hour or so. During that time, observe him or her carefully, finding out all you can, watching gestures and expressions, as well as physical features. Talk with the person, asking about likes and dislikes or important issues.

Should have done.

Then write as clear and specific a description of this person as you can. You may organize your paper as you did for the in-class writing with one paragraph on the face, a second on the body, and a third on the personality. You may want to have just two paragraphs — one on physical appearance and another on personality. Or you may prefer three paragraphs, covering what the person looks like, what the person does, and what you think of him or her.

Checklist for Use before Writing Final Draft

1. Were the words you used specific and clear?
2. Did you avoid problem words like *good, nice,* and *medium?*
3. Which of the three plans did you use to organize your description?

4. Did you include interesting information about the person you described?
5. How many times did you have to rewrite this piece before you were satisfied?

Chapter Two

Describing an Object

Our lives are filled with objects. We walk by them and occasionally we bump into them. We touch them, hold them, and sometimes drop them. We sit on them, stand on them, lie on them or in them. We also smell them and see them. We even taste them. We do all this very automatically without ever fully noticing the details of the many objects that surround us. In this chapter, you will have an opportunity to experience and enjoy objects as you strengthen your ability to focus on *specific details*. In addition, you will discover that to get the details a vivid description needs, you must use your five senses. You will also find out how the use of comparison can enrich your writing.

Remember that you can write a good description only in the presence of the object you're describing. Don't trust your memory of how a thing looks, feels, tastes, or smells. Your memory is apt to play surprising tricks on you, as the following dialogue shows.

Teacher Think of an apple. It's round and red, and tastes good, right?

Class Right!

Teacher Wrong! Look at this apple. Is it red?

Student A Well, . . . yes and no.

Teacher What do you mean by that?

Student A Well, it's mostly red, but there is a little green on one side.

Student B And the red's not the same red all over — in some places the red's so dark, it's almost black and in other places it's a much lighter red — like the red of a tomato.

Teacher   And what about the green portion?

Student A   Well, that's not all green either — it's got patches of pale green and yellow.

Student C   Come to think of it, it's not round either.

Teacher   Then what shape is it?

Student A   It's kind of pushed in at the top and the bottom, and it's broader at the top than at the bottom.

Student C   Actually, it's shaped like a heart with its tip pushed in, if you know what I mean.

Student B   To me it looks more like the shape of a head seen from the front.

Teacher   Then it's not round like a tennis ball?

Student A   No, but it sure tastes good! Especially when you're hungry.

Student C   Yeah, I love that tart taste.

Student A   No, I hate that kind. I like the sweet ones.

Student B   And I hate all apples!

Very often, as in the instance above, we describe things so vaguely that we end up not describing them at all. This happens when we describe objects by what we've heard about them. We tend to take our senses for granted or even forget we have them. But if we think about it, our senses have already played a very important role in our lives. All of us learned our first lessons before we knew how to read, write, or speak. And we learned them through our senses of sight, touch, taste, smell, and hearing. Because one of the basic purposes of writing is to communicate what we observe and experience through our senses, it is now necessary for us to reawaken our senses and put them back into use. Both our writing and our experience can be enriched by this.

ACTIVITY   Using Your Senses to Choose Significant Detail   Put an object from your pocket or pocketbook into a brown paper bag.

Part I

Volunteer 1   Put on a blindfold. Pick an object from the bag and describe it to the class. Tell what it feels, sounds, smells, and, if possible, even what it tastes like. Then try to guess what the object is.

Volunteer 2   While Volunteer 1 is describing the object, write on the board all the words and phrases he or she uses, grouping them according to the sense they refer to. For example, if Volunteer 1 says the object is rough, write "rough" under "sense of touch."

Class When Volunteer 1 has guessed or failed to guess what the object is, discuss how accurate and specific his or her perceptions were. What other sense details could have been used to describe the object?

Part II

Volunteer 3 Do not put on a blindfold. Pick another object from the bag with your back to the class so the class cannot see the object. Describe it in as much detail as you can, saying what the object feels, tastes, smells, sounds as well as looks like until the class is able to guess what it is. The class may ask you questions to clarify or add to your description.

Class Discuss how the use of sight helped to make the description more clear and complete. Add any new words or phrases dealing with the senses to the proper sense group on the board.

Part III

Now divide into groups of five. Each member in the group chooses one sense to work with. Blindfold two members of the group; for example, the two who chose smell and hearing in one group, the two who chose touch and taste in another and so on. The persons who chose sight in all groups, of course, cannot be blindfolded.

Each group pick one object from the bag, making sure the other groups cannot see it. Pass the object around in your group. List all the qualities you notice about the object *with the sense you are working with*. For instance, if you are working with the sense of sound, drop the object on the floor, knock it against the wooden or plastic back of your chair, against its steel legs, against a wall, and write down what it sounds like.

IN-CLASS WRITING

Writing a Group Description of an Object When your group is finished, pool your information and write a group description of your object.

Choose one member of your group to read the description to the class. After the other groups have had a chance to guess what the object is, pass it around. Are there any things you could add or change in your description to make it more clear and complete?

Discussion

1. By focusing on your senses, what new qualities of the object did you discover?
2. Did you find new words to describe the particular sort of smoothness or roughness of the object?
3. Did you find new words to describe a particular color, shape, sound, or smell?

Comparing Objects   You will have noticed that quite often you used phrases like:

1. _____ feels as smooth as glass.
2. _____ tastes like a raw potato.
3. _____ is shaped like a baseball.

What you did was to compare a particular quality of another object more familiar to you with a similar quality of the object in hand. When you use a comparison, you generally do this with the help of the words "like" and "as."

Comparisons are useful in making descriptions more specific and concrete, and they help to express feelings and ideas more clearly and vividly.

For instance, T. S. Eliot describes the evening in his poem "Love Song of J. Alfred Prufrock" by comparing it to a patient:

Let us go then, you and I,
When the evening is spread out against the sky
Like a patient etherized upon a table.

Langston Hughes describes an unfulfilled dream in his poem "Harlem" by two comparisons.

What happens to a dream deferred?

Does it dry up
like a raisin in the sun?

Or fester like a sore —
And then run?

It is also possible to make a comparison without using the words "like" or "as."

Example: Jessica is a blooming peony.

This does not mean that Jessica is a flower and not a person. A peony is a big, rather dramatic flower that is also delicate and soft. It is the qualities of bigness, drama, delicacy, and softness in Jessica that remind you of the peony.

Langston Hughes' poem, "Mother to Son," compares the life of a woman to a climbing staircase.

Well, son, I'll tell you:
Life for me ain't been no crystal stair.
It's had tacks in it,
And splinters,
And boards torn up,
And places with no carpets on the floor —
Bare.
But all the time
I's been a-climbin' on,
And reachin' landin's,
And turnin' corners,
And sometimes goin' in the dark
Where there ain't been no light,
So boy, don't you turn back,
Don't you set down on the steps
Cause you finds it kinder hard.
Don't you fall now —
For I's still goin', honey,
I's still climbin'
And life for me ain't been no crystal stair.

ACTIVITY　**Expressing Your Thoughts and Feelings**　Descriptions of people, places or things become even more interesting when you describe not only their physical and sensory qualities but also when you communicate what you think and how you feel about them.

In the last activity, you focused on the physical qualities of things. In the next one, you will use things to express how you think and feel about a person.

In this activity, you will try to discover the essence of each other; in other words, not what each of you *looks* like, but rather what kind of person you seem to *be* to the others in the room.

Directions

Write several categories of objects on the board, for example: flowers, fruits, animals, buildings, furniture, cars, clothing, beverages, foods, musical groups, and any others you think of.

Select one student to leave the classroom for a minute. The rest of you choose one person in the room whose essence you will describe with reference to the categories on the board.

Then ask the volunteer to come in. He or she asks individual students questions like, If this student is a building, what kind of building is he or she? Your answers must indicate why you associate the person with a particular building. For example, you might say, He is a tower because he is tall and strong. The volunteer may ask three questions before attempting to guess the identity of the chosen person.

It may happen that the volunteer is unable to guess, but this does not mean that anyone is "wrong." Rather, it shows that each of you has unique personal impressions of people and things that are based on your own experiences and associations.

Discussion

1. When you heard someone describing the person chosen as a tower or black coffee, for example, would you have used another kind of building or beverage? Why?
2. Did the answers for each person who was chosen reveal a common quality?
3. What does this tell you about the perceiver and the person perceived?

IN-CLASS WRITING   **Writing Subjective and Objective Descriptions** As you have seen, examining something with all of your senses adds to the completeness of your descriptions and using comparisons helps to clarify exactly how something looks, tastes, feels, smells, or sounds. Comparisons can also communicate what you think or feel about what you are describing.

There are essentially two ways of describing what you observe — you can describe something either *objectively* or *subjectively*. When you describe objectively, you record what you observe impersonally — that is, with as much precision and accuracy as you can, without telling how you feel about it. For example, if you were writing a report for your science teacher about the cells you observed under a microscope, you would obviously have to describe them objectively: their shape, color, texture, movement. When you describe something subjectively, you not only paint a verbal picture but you color it with your personal feelings and responses. If you were telling your friend about your science class later that evening, you might add how sick you felt watching those slippery, slimy creatures swimming about under your eye. However, subjective and objective descriptions are often combined.

Write a description of something you have with you in class today. You might describe one of your shoes, a book, your pocketbook, your glasses, your ring, or anything you have which you find interesting enough to write about.

Organize your paper as follows: In the first part of your paper, write an objective description of the item. There will be two sections in this part. In the first section, your goal will be to communicate accurately what the object looks like. Write about the item's size, shape, weight, color, and texture. For example, if you are describing your wallet, you could say it is a small, grey, leather rectangle 4½ inches long and 2½ inches wide. You might also add that when it is empty it looks no larger than a pack of king-sized cigarettes, but because it is usually so stuffed it appears to be as thick as Webster's Unabridged Dictionary.

In the second section, explore the object with your other senses. Write about how it feels, sounds, tastes, and smells. To do this, test the object. Touch it, squeeze it, smell it, roll it. For example, you might discover that when you throw your wallet on the floor it makes a dull thumping sound somewhat like the thud of someone running in wet sneakers. Do everything necessary to discover whatever you can about it and then share your discoveries on paper.

In the second part of your paper, write a subjective description of the object. Here you will tell how you feel about the object. You might say that you think of your wallet as an old friend and that you remember the sad times when it was too thin and the happier times when it made a fat bulge in your pocket.

You may have noticed as you participated in the sense activity and the comparison activity that sometimes you found it difficult to guess what the object or who the person was because the object or the person had not been described completely — in other words, important details had been omitted. Every composition, whether it is a story, a painting, a song, or even an outfit, needs sufficient detail if you want the viewer, the reader, the listener and even the buyer to appreciate it.

Read the passage below:

ZEN AND THE ART OF MOTORCYCLE MAINTENANCE — Robert M. Pirsig

. . . He'd been having trouble with students who had nothing to say. At first he thought it was laziness but later it became apparent that it wasn't. They just couldn't think of anything to say.

One of them, a girl with strong-lensed glasses, wanted to write a five-hundred-word essay about the United States. He was used to the sinking feeling that comes from statements like this, and suggested without disparagement that she narrow it down to just Bozeman.

When the paper came due she didn't have it and was quite upset. She had tried and tried but she just couldn't think of anything to say. . . .

It just stumped him. Now *he* couldn't think of anything to say. A silence occurred, and then a peculiar answer: "Narrow it down to the *main street* of Bozeman." It was a stroke of insight.

She nodded dutifully and went out. But just before her next class she came back in *real* distress, tears this time, distress that had obviously been there for a long time. She still couldn't think of anything to say, and couldn't understand why, if she couldn't think of anything about all of Bozeman, she should be able to think of something about just one street.

He was furious. "You're not *looking!*" he said. . . . She really wasn't looking and yet somehow didn't understand this. He told her angrily, "Narrow it down to the *front* of one building on the main street of Bozeman. The Opera House. Start with the upper left-hand brick."

Her eyes, behind the thick-lensed glasses, opened wide.

She came in the next class with a puzzled look and

handed him a five-thousand-word essay on the front of the Opera House on the main street of Bozeman, Montana. "I sat in the hamburger stand across the street," she said, "and started writing about the first brick and the second brick, and then by the third brick it all started to come and I couldn't stop. They thought I was crazy, and they kept kidding me, but here it all is. I don't understand it."

Neither did he, but on long walks through the streets of town he thought about it and concluded she was evidently stopped with the same kind of blockage that had paralyzed him on his first day of teaching. She was blocked because she was trying to repeat, in her writing, things she had already heard, just as on the first day he had tried to repeat things he had already decided to say. She couldn't think of anything to write about Bozeman because she couldn't recall anything she had heard worth repeating. She was strangely unaware that she could look and see freshly for herself, as she wrote, without primary regard for what had been said before. The narrowing down to one brick destroyed the blockage because it was so obvious that she *had* to do some original and direct seeing.

Discussion

1. What was the student's problem?
2. Why was the girl's discovery a useful one?
3. What have you learned from her experience?
4. What problems might she now have as she writes her paper on the bricks of the building?

A very important quality of a good description is *detail*. However, a detailed description does not have to include every single thing you observe about your subject. It is the significant details — the details that give that subject its uniqueness and particularity — that make descriptions effective. For example, if you wish to describe a person who attracted your attention at a party, think about why he or she attracted you. Was it because this person had the most beautiful face, wore the most outrageous clothes, had a very musical voice and a lilting laugh, or gestured very effusively? Zero in on those qualities and describe them in careful detail. If the height, build, or figure were not particularly striking, you will not want to spend much time on them.

DESCRIBING A PICTURE

On the facing page is a photograph depicting an old house. Look at it carefully so that you can answer the questions that follow.

Discussion

1. If you were writing a description of an old house, what would you include? Why?
2. What would you leave out? Why?

Now that you know that an effective description must have significant details in clear, precise, and vivid words, you are almost ready to write a good description — but not quite. How are you going to arrange or order all your material so that your readers can visualize in their mind's eye exactly what you are describing? Organization is necessary in all kinds of writing. Without it your readers will throw up their hands in despair because you have created scattered impressions. But you need not despair; organizing your details is not difficult — it is a matter of common sense. If you are describing a person, for example, you would normally go from top (head) to bottom (feet), or from the general (the figure) to the particular (the face, the body, the limbs), or from the outside (physical appearance) to the inside (personality) or vice versa. The same methods can be used to describe an object. If, on the other hand, you are describing a landscape, you might go from near to far, or far to near, left to right, or right to left, or from the most striking to the less striking features of the subject of your description.

Person

1. head
   a. hair (color, texture, shape)
   b. face (shape, eyes, nose, mouth)
   c. neck
2. body
   a. top: chest
   b. bottom: hips
3. limbs
   a. arms and hands
   b. legs and feet

Landscape

1. far
   a. sun
   b. mountains
2. middle
   a. house
   b. tree
   c. end of path
3. near
   a. cat
   b. flowers
   c. start of path

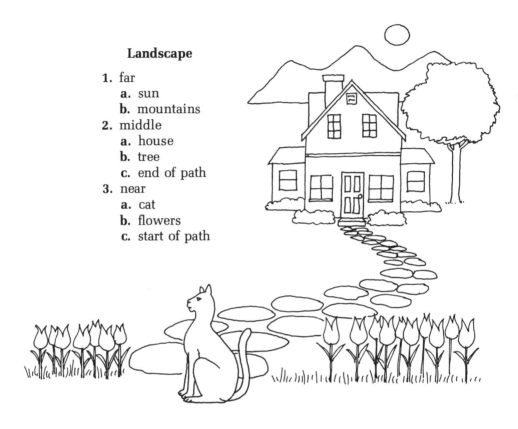

Describing the Face of a Building   Your city or town has many buildings, most of which are different from one another. These are the buildings each of you live in or shop in or see the dentist in. Each of these buildings has a front — a face — and it is one of those faces that you will describe for this writing assignment.

Select a building that has a front that interests you. Observe and inspect the front of that building as thoroughly and as carefully as you can. Then write a complete description of the front of that building. Be sure to decide on one plan of organization and stick with it throughout the paper.

Checklist for Use before Writing Final Draft

1. Have you established a principle of organization and stuck to that principle of organization throughout your description?

2. Have you as accurately as possible presented the facts about the front of the building you are describing?

3. Have you emphasized the significant details of the front of the building?

4. Were the words you chose to describe the front of the building accurate and precise?

5. Have you used your senses to enrich your description?

6. Have you used comparisons to clarify what the front of the building is like?

7. Have you used comparisons to convey your thoughts and feelings about the front of the building you described?

8. Is your description thorough and complete?

Chapter Three

Describing a Place: Sensing Your Neighborhood

In this chapter, you will be asked to do two things: to walk and to look. Obviously, you have been doing these things for quite some time; but how many times have you actually concentrated on either or on both? Have you ever walked and thought only of the fact that you were walking? Have you ever looked at something and concentrated not so much on the object of your gaze as on yourself in the act of looking?

These questions are important because by asking them you are indirectly asking yourself about your awareness of what you do and what you see. You may first ask, however, What is awareness? Has anyone ever asked you to define it? Where did you begin? Perhaps you began by naming the five senses. Perhaps you explained how your senses inform you about the state of the world outside yourself so that you can make appropriate decisions regarding it. For example, you feel cold and you put on a fur or wool garment; it is hot and you want to swim, so you put on a bikini. You wear dark glasses in bright sunlight, and you blink, widening your eyes as you walk into a darkened room. Awareness begins with your five senses, your perceptions. The world around you bombards you with stimuli. Through your five senses you react to these stimuli: colors, voices, an embrace, a bowl of chili, a lilac bush, a rat.

ACTIVITY   **Learning to Focus**   To help develop your awareness, practise focusing on an object like a matchstick or a cigarette. See it as though it were the only thing existing except for you who are its observer. It is as if you have brought it into existence; your awareness of it has *made* it exist. When you have finished, consider whether or not you have discovered any new attributes in a matchstick or a cigarette. Were all five senses operating? Now, for the next few moments, close your eyes and concentrate on yourself. Imagine that you are at the center of the universe, or, to go one step farther, imagine you *are* the center of the universe. Imagine then all the things that are happening within yourself. You are the observer and the observed, immersed in the act of observing. Now, open your eyes. Jot down the impressions you were most keenly aware of. As other students are reading aloud their impressions, compare what you experienced with what they experienced.

Discussion

1. In that moment or two of focusing, how many of your senses were you using?
2. Because you were focusing, did you feel your awareness was increased? Try to explain.
3. What value did closing your eyes lend to your ability to focus?
4. Do you think it's possible for you to achieve the same level of awareness with your eyes open?
5. What value do you think there is in learning to focus? What value can it have to the process of writing?

IN-CLASS WRITING **Recording Perceptions** Develop into a paragraph five things you jotted down. Make sure you weave into your observations your own comments on what discoveries you made during this brief experiment.

ACTIVITY **Taking a Walk in Your Neighborhood** The following are a series of activities designed to assist you in becoming more aware of the things that are — and happen — around you and, additionally, to sharpen your vocabulary so that you can record to your satisfaction the things you have seen, heard and felt.

Part I
You will now take a healthy leap from focusing briefly in on your awareness of what is going on around you in your

classroom (with your eyes closed) to a long, leisurely walk down your block and around a corner or two (with your eyes wide open). Consider the number of times you've walked the length and breadth of the block you live on and the streets that run perpendicular to it, just above and just below the house or apartment building you live in. How many times have you walked or run up and down these streets? Yet has it ever occurred to you just how much you've actually seen, heard, felt, smelled? Have you ever noticed anything special about your block? In how many ways could you distinguish it from any other town or city block? Are you uniquely different from any other person you've ever met or seen? If you are, is that uniqueness related to where you live? These are the kinds of questions you might mull over when, bright and early Saturday morning, you take your first walk around your neighborhood. On this walk, you are going to open up your five senses and let the stimuli waft into your consciousness. Don't force anything to happen, just walk and be relaxed in the activity itself. For this first experimental and experiential walk of, say, about 20 minutes, let the enjoyment of the stimuli as they press into your consciousness take over. When you get back home, jot down about three or four significant impressions you recall. These impressions you write down are for your own personal records. Your list of impressions might look something like this:

1. Why does everybody who passes that old mutt of the Stokeses jump out of its way? It hasn't got a tooth in its head.
2. Counted eight discarded beer cans just from my house to the corner of Park Street. Five were Molson's; is this the beer Canadians love most?
3. Are those real wildflowers in the vacant lot next to Mr. Alvarez's Pizza Hut or are they just weeds with frizzled blue blossoms?
4. I wonder who went off and left that '57 Pontiac in front of Marion's house. There's a copy of Consumer magazine on the back seat.

Now, look over what you have written and check it against these questions:

1. By not thinking of anything in particular, did you experience a greater awareness of where you were and what you were doing?

2. Did your senses seem to be operating more efficiently, or were you just more responsive to them?

Part II

Either later in the same day or early Sunday morning, take a second walk. This time you will be deliberately focusing. Here, be more aware of what your senses tell you. You can call it a sensory trip, because you will consciously exercise your senses, which, in turn, will automatically heighten your awareness of what you are seeing, hearing, feeling, smelling. (If you want to exercise your taste, buy a pizza, a hot dog, or drink a Coke or a cup of coffee, and devour it with zest!) When you get home, rummage through the imagery you collected while walking. What do you remember most? What things stand out most sharply?

Now, get out your paper and pencil and write a list of twenty objects you recall most vividly. Remember, however, this is a list of *things*. Use a minimum of descriptive words; they will come later. You are being a materialist; you are only concerned with objects. Now, you are ready to bring your list to class and read it to the group. Your list just might look something like this:

1. 6 beer cans	11. playground
2. weeds in a lot	12. a pizza slice
3. car with no wheels or engine	13. "No Parking" signs
4. pizza parlor	14. two oak trees
5. church	15. a dog named Peter
6. parkside	16. *Consumer* magazine
7. bay windows	17. frame house
8. row houses	18. a kitchen sink
9. hospital	19. a statue in a park
10. sewing machine	20. a preacher

Discussion

1. Having gone through the first two activities of this chapter, what can you say that you are learning about *focusing* and *awareness*?
2. In what ways do you think focusing broadens and deepens awareness? Maybe you don't think focusing affects awareness at all; if so, why not?
3. What value did you find in taking your two walks? Explain.
4. Suppose you had gotten into a car and had driven around these blocks, would you have had the same impressions? In what ways would they have been different?

Identifying Elements of the Sentence Words and grammar are everybody's property. You each have your private stock that you share with other speakers of English. Every time you speak you dip into that private stock of yours so that you can communicate to another person. Each of you has between 10 000 and 20 000 words that you draw on daily. The twenty things you listed while walking named things or objects with words called nouns. Nouns are important because they become subjects of sentences.

Later on in this chapter you will be asked to use your list of twenty objects, add modifiers to them, and construct ten sentences. But before you do so, you should review the main elements that make up a sentence.

There are many definitions of the sentence, but the one most students have memorized at some time goes like this: *A sentence is a group of words that has a subject and a verb and expresses a complete thought.* You have probably heard this definition or one like it. In order to make it useful, you have to understand the three key elements — subject, verb, and complete thought.

The Subject

Look at the following sentence: *John laughed.* It is only two words long yet it is a complete and correct sentence. In this sentence, the word *John* is the subject. It is the focus of the sentence and answers the question "Who laughed?" The subject of a sentence is usually a noun (a word that names a person, place, or thing) or a pronoun (a word that substitutes for a noun). Words like *man, house, birds, guitar, democracy* are all nouns and can be subjects of sentences. Words like *he, she, you, we, they* are all pronouns, and they too can be subjects of sentences. The word *John*, for instance, could be changed to *he*. The sentence would then be: *He laughed.* There is less information here, but there is still enough to know that the sentence is focused on some unspecified man and there is an answer to the question *Who laughed?*

The subject is the focus of the sentence.

The subject is usually a noun (a word that names a person, place, or thing) or a pronoun (a word that substitutes for a noun).

The subject of the sentence tells who or what did the action of the verb.

The Verb

The word *laughed* is the verb of the sentence. The verb is the word that tells the action of the sentence. *Jump, run, sing, laugh* are verbs, and they are so familiar to you that you have no trouble recognizing them as action words. There is another group of verbs, however, that might cause some trouble. These verbs, such as *am, is, are, was, were, seems, feels* convey very little sense of action, but they are nonetheless verbs. If you have trouble recognizing them, you will have to spend a few minutes memorizing them. Another group of verbs that do not seem to involve physical action are words like *think, consider, advise, refuse.* You can't see the action taking place because it is going on inside you, but if you recall how tired you were after studying for an exam, you will realize how much action *thinking* represents. Some students mistake words like *to* and *in* for verbs. These words tell the direction of the action, but they don't specify that action. In the sentence *John ran to school,* the word *to* tells you where John went (the direction) but it doesn't tell you how he went.

The verb is the word that expresses the action of the sentence. It tells you what happened.

Recognizing a complete thought in the examples given above was not difficult but there are a few other cases where you might have trouble. Some verbs need an extra word to give completeness. In the sentence *Mary grabbed the pencil* the word *pencil* is necessary to complete the thought. In the same way you would need additional words to make sense in the following cases: *The book seems easy. The bed feels soft. The train was late.*

Still another problem occurs when the verb has more than one word in it. If you write *John was running to school,* the verb of the sentence becomes *was running,* not just *running.* Verbs ending in *-ing* need a helping or auxiliary verb in order to be the main verb of the sentence. These helping verb forms — *have, had, has, was, were, can, will, shall, do, does, did* — are as necessary for some sentences as the form that you recognize as the action word.

The Linking Word

While some problems exist because a sentence may not be complete, there is also a problem that a sentence can be over-complete — that is, there is more than one main subject-verb unit.

For instance, you might write a sentence like this one: *Mary studied all week, she got an A on her chemistry test.* Looking at this sentence, you can see that there are two subject-verb units, each expressing a complete thought: *Mary studied all week* and *she got an A on her chemistry test.* You can only have one such unit to a sentence unless you use a linking word like *because, although, since* to join a second unit to the first. These sentences are called run-ons, fused sentences, or comma splices.

In order to achieve completeness in a sentence, you may need an extra word after the verb or you may need a helping verb; but you can only have one main subject-verb unit unless you use a linking word.

The Modifier

If you only wrote and thought in two- and three-word sentences, your life and your writing would be very dull. Fortunately, your thought processes and your vocabulary are far broader. Looking back at the original sentence, *John laughed,* you can probably think of a number of additions you might want to add. These additional words are called modifiers, which means that they qualify, alter, restrict, or otherwise change the meaning not just of nouns, but other words as well. Modifiers are useful because they bring color, variety, and specificity to your writing. When used imaginatively, they literally activate the eye and mind of the reader.

Think now of how *John* looked. Perhaps he was short, plump, and jolly. If we add these modifiers to our sentence, it would read: *Short, plump, jolly John laughed.* Now you might want to describe how he laughed. Was it uproariously? Where was he when this was happening? At the zoo? Why? Was it because the monkeys were making faces at the people? If you put all these ideas together, the sentence would come out like this: *Short, plump, jolly John laughed uproariously at the zoo because the monkeys were making faces at the people.* The original two-word sentence has now been expanded to eighteen words.

Let us return to your lists of twenty objects. Your lists name things that have *concreteness.* By concreteness, we mean that which we can experience through one or more of our senses, most notably that which we can see and touch, or which can make a sound when we strike or drop it. Concreteness, then, denotes that which has mass, size, breadth, depth, density, color, texture, and so on. The point we are emphasizing here is that each list should name objects — twenty *concrete* nouns.

Now add modifiers to these concrete things. You will be adding to your reader's understanding of those objects. Through these modifiers, your reader too will be able to fully sense the objects you have collected.

Listed below are some sentences and phrases that show how modifiers work and, in fact, how much of a sentence consists of modifying words. As you can see, modifiers answer such important questions as, Which? What kind? How?

1. We live *in an old two-storey red-brick* house *that had been vacant for years.*
2. The house was *decidedly not worth buying.*
3. *Helen's* face, *etched with lines of age, weariness, and exhaustion,* cheered *just for a moment.*
4. It was *an old blue car left for the strippers and vandalizers.*
5. I saw *a stately old* elm *that seemed half hidden between two apartment buildings.*

Exercise

Either individually or as a class decide on a subject-verb core and see how many modifiers you can add.

Writing Sentences about Your Neighborhood Write ten sentences using all twenty objects or as many as you can without straining the point. The sentences need not be organized for any special effect. They should reflect, however, things that you looked at during your walk. Look at the following sentences to see what you might like to do when you write your own sentences:

1. My neighborhood consists mostly of row houses; some go straight up; others protrude with bay windows on the third floor.
2. Maybe you could guess the kind of neighborhood you're in by the kinds of things people throw away; for example, beer cans, a kitchen sink, a sewing machine.
3. Peter is a dog who belongs to our neighbors two houses down, and he looks fearsome enough to bite anybody who passes if you don't know that he hasn't got any teeth.

4. My neighborhood has services that nourish body, mind, and soul, which means we have a hospital, a school, and a church.
5. When I stand at my gate, I can look up at the park at the end of the block. The benches facing it are always occupied on warm days.
6. Alvarez's Pizza Hut across from the parkside bathes the passerby with its own special kind of aroma.
7. The only frame house in the whole area is a real museum piece. It hasn't been lived in since I was a kid.
8. Our hospital looks like a set for a Dracula movie.
9. Those flowers in the vacant lot next to Alvarez's Pizza Hut might just be weeds, but their blue blossoms are very pretty to look at.
10. I can't help wondering why a stripped '57 Pontiac has a copy of *Consumer* on the back seat.

READING The story that follows, Eudora Welty's "A Worn Path," is rich in description. The main character, Aunt Phoenix, comes alive to us from the pages; her world is spread open before us in a way that all of our senses participate in the old woman's pilgrimage through the Mississippi woods to the town of Natchez.

A WORN PATH — Eudora Welty

It was December — a bright frozen day in the early morning. Far out in the country there was an old Negro woman with her head tied in a red rag, coming along a path through the pinewoods. Her name was Phoenix Jackson. She was very old and small and she walked slowly in the dark pine shadows, moving a little from side to side in her steps, with the balanced heaviness and lightness of a pendulum in a grandfather clock. She carried a thin, small cane made from an umbrella, and with this she kept tapping the frozen earth in front of her. This made a grave and persistent noise in the still air, that seemed meditative, like the chirping of a solitary little bird.

She wore a dark striped dress reaching down to her shoe-tops, and an equally long apron of bleached sugar sacks, with a full pocket; all neat and tidy, but every time she took a step she might have fallen over her shoelaces, which dragged from her unlaced shoes. She looked straight ahead. Her eyes were blue with age. Her skin had a pattern all its own of numberless branching wrinkles and as though a whole little tree stood in the middle of her forehead, but a golden color ran underneath, and the two knobs of her cheeks were illuminated by a yellow burning under the dark. Under the red rag her hair came down on her neck in the frailest of ringlets, still black, and with an odor like copper.

Now and then there was a quivering in the thicket. Old Phoenix said, "Out of my way, all you foxes, owls, beetles, jack rabbits, coons, and wild animals! . . . Keep out from under these feet, little bobwhites. . . . Keep the big wild hogs out of my path. Don't let none of those come running my direction. I got a long way." Under her small black-freckled hand her cane, limber as a buggy whip, would switch at the brush as if to rouse up any hiding things.

On she went. The woods were deep and still. The sun made the pine needles almost too bright to look at, up where the wind rocked. The cones dropped as light as feathers. Down in the hollow was the mourning dove — it was not too late for him.

The path ran up a hill. "Seem like there is chains about my feet, time I get this far," she said, in the voice of argument old people keep to use with themselves. "Something always take a hold on this hill — pleads I should stay."

After she got to the top she turned and gave a full, severe look behind her where she had come. "Up through pines," she said at length. "Now down through oaks."

Her eyes opened their widest and she started down gently. But before she got to the bottom of the hill a bush caught her dress.

Her fingers were busy and intent, but her skirts were full and long, so that before she could pull them free in one place they were caught in another. It was not possible to allow the dress to tear. "I in the thorny bush," she said. "Thorns, you doing your appointed work. Never want to let folks past — no sir. Old eyes thought you was a pretty little green bush."

Finally, trembling all over, she stood free, and after a moment dared to stoop for her cane.

"Sun so high!" she cried, leaning back and looking, while the thick tears went over her eyes. "The time getting all gone here."

At the foot of this hill was a place where a log was laid across the creek.

"Now comes the trial," said Phoenix.

Putting her right foot out, she mounted the log and shut her eyes. Lifting her skirt, leveling her cane fiercely before her, like a festival figure in some parade, she began to march across. Then she opened her eyes and she was safe on the other side.

"I wasn't as old as I thought," she said.

But she sat down to rest. She spread her skirts on the bank around her and folded her hands over her knees. Up above her was a tree in a pearly cloud of mistletoe. She did not dare to close her eyes, and when a little boy brought her a little plate with a slice of marble-cake on it she spoke to him. "That would be acceptable," she said. But when she went to take it there was just her own hand in the air.

So she left that tree, and had to go through a barbed-wire fence. There she had to creep and crawl, spreading her knees and stretching her fingers like a baby trying to climb the steps. But she talked loudly to herself; she could not let her dress be torn now, so late in the day, and she could not pay for having her arm or her leg sawed off if she got caught fast where she was.

At last she was safe through the fence and risen up out in the clearing. Big dead trees, like black men with one arm, were standing in the purple stalks of the withered cotton field. There sat a buzzard.

"Who you watching?"

In the furrow she made her way along.

"Glad this not the season for bulls," she said, looking sideways, "and the good Lord made his snakes to curl up and sleep in the winter. A pleasure I don't see no two-headed snake coming around that tree, where it come once. It took a while to get by him, back in the summer."

She passed through the old cotton and went into a field of dead corn. It whispered and shook, and was taller than her head. "Through the maze now," she said, for there was no path.

Then there was something tall, black, and skinny there, moving before her.

At first she took it for a man. It could have been a man dancing in the field. But she stood still and listened, and it did not make a sound. It was as silent as a ghost.

"Ghost," she said sharply, "who be you the ghost of? For I have heard of nary death close by."

But there was no answer, only the ragged dancing in the wind.

She shut her eyes, reached out her hand, and touched a sleeve. She found a coat and inside that an emptiness, cold as ice.

"You scarecrow," she said. Her face lighted. "I ought to be shut up for good," she said with laughter. "My senses is gone. I too old. I the oldest people I ever know. Dance, old scarecrow," she said, "while I dancing with you."

She kicked her foot over the furrow, and with mouth drawn down shook her head once or twice in a little strutting way. Some husks blew down and whirled in streamers about her skirts.

Then she went on, parting her way from side to side with the cane, through the whispering field. At last she came to the end, to a wagon track, where the silver grass blew between the red ruts. The quail were walking around like pullets, seeming all dainty and unseen.

"Walk pretty," she said. "This the easy place. This the easy going."

She followed the track, swaying through the quiet bare fields, through the little strings of trees silver in their dead leaves, past cabins silver from weather, with the doors and windows boarded shut, all like old women under a spell sitting there. "I walking in their sleep," she said, nodding her head vigorously.

In a ravine she went where a spring was silently flowing through a hollow log. Old Phoenix bent and drank. "Sweetgum makes the water sweet," she said, and drank more. "Nobody knows who made this well, for it was here when I was born."

The track crossed a swampy part where the moss hung as white as lace from every limb. "Sleep on, alligators, and blow your bubbles." Then the track went into the road.

Deep, deep the road went down between the high green-colored banks. Overhead the live-oaks met, and it was as dark as a cave.

A black dog with a lolling tongue came up out of the weeds by the ditch. She was meditating, and not ready, and when he came at her she only hit him a little with her cane. Over she went in the ditch, like a little puff of milk-weed.

Down there, her senses drifted away. A dream visited

her, and she reached her hand up, but nothing reached down and gave her a pull. So she lay there and presently went to talking. "Old woman," she said to herself, "that black dog come up out of the weeds to stall you off, and now there he sitting on his fine tail, smiling at you."

A white man finally came along and found her — a hunter, a young man, with his dog on a chain.

"Well, Granny!" he laughed. "What are you doing there?"

"Lying on my back like a June-bug waiting to be turned over, mister," she said, reaching up her hand.

He lifted her up, gave her a swing in the air, and set her down, "Anything broken, Granny?"

"No sir, them old dead weeds is springy enough," said Phoenix, when she had got her breath. "I thank you for your trouble."

"Where do you live, Granny?" he asked, while the two dogs were growling at each other.

"Away back yonder, sir, behind the ridge. You can't even see it from here."

"On your way home?"

"No, sir, I going to town."

"Why, that's too far! That's as far as I walk when I come out myself, and I get something for my trouble." He patted the stuffed bag he carried, and there hung down a little closed claw. It was one of the bobwhites, with its beak hooked bitterly to show it was dead. "Now you go on home, Granny!"

"I bound to go to town, mister," said Phoenix. "The time come around."

He gave another laugh, filling the whole landscape. "I know you colored people! Wouldn't miss going to town to see Santa Claus!"

But something held Old Phoenix very still. The deep lines in her face went into a fierce and different radiation. Without warning she had seen with her own eyes a flashing nickel fall out of the man's pocket on to the ground.

"How old are you, Granny?" he was saying.

"There is no telling, mister," she said, "no telling."

Then she gave a little cry and clapped her hands, and said, "Git on away from here, dog! Look! Look at that dog!" She laughed as if in admiration. "He ain't scared of nobody. He a big black dog." She whispered, "Sick him!"

"Watch me get rid of that cur," said the man. "Sick him. Pete! Sick him!"

Phoenix heard the dogs fighting and heard the man running and throwing sticks. She even heard a gunshot. But she was slowly bending forward by that time, further and further forward, the lids stretched down over her eyes, as if she were doing this in her sleep. Her chin was lowered almost to her knees. The yellow palm of her hand came out from the fold of her apron. Her fingers slid down and along the ground under the piece of money with the grace and care they would have in lifting an egg from under a sitting hen. Then she slowly straightened up, she stood erect, and the nickel was in her apron pocket. A bird flew by. Her lips moved. "God watching me the whole time. I come to stealing."

The man came back, and his own dog panted about them. "Well, I scared him off that time," he said, and then he laughed and lifted his gun and pointed it at Phoenix.

She stood straight and faced him.

"Doesn't the gun scare you?" he said, still pointing it.

"No, sir, I seen plenty go off closer by, in my day, and for less than what I done," she said, holding utterly still.

He smiled, and shouldered the gun. "Well, Granny," he said, "you must be a hundred years old, and scared of nothing. I'd give you a dime if I had any money with me. But you take my advice and stay home, and nothing will happen to you."

"I bound to go on my way, mister," said Phoenix. She inclined her head in the red rag. Then they went in different directions, but she could hear the gun shooting again and again over the hill.

She walked on. The shadows hung from the oak trees to the road like curtains. Then she smelled wood-smoke, and smelled the river, and she saw a steeple and the cabins on their steep steps. Dozens of little black children whirled around her. There ahead was Natchez shining. Bells were ringing. She walked on.

In the paved city it was Christmas time. There were red and green electric lights strung and crisscrossed everywhere, and all turned on in the daytime. Old Phoenix would have been lost if she had not distrusted her eyesight and depended on her feet to know where to take her.

She paused quietly on the sidewalk, where people were

passing by. A lady came along in the crowd, carrying an armful of red-, green-, and silver-wrapped presents; she gave off perfume like the red roses in hot summer, and Phoenix stopped her.

"Please, missy, will you lace up my shoe?" She held up her foot.

"What do you want, Grandma?"

"See my shoe," said Phoenix. "Do all right for out in the country, but wouldn't look right to go in a big building."

"Stand still then, Grandma," said the lady. She put her packages down carefully on the sidewalk beside her and laced and tied both shoes tightly.

"Can't lace 'em with a cane," said Phoenix. "Thank you, missy. I doesn't mind asking a nice lady to tie up my shoe when I gets out on the street."

Moving slowly and from side to side, she went into the stone building and into a tower of steps, where she walked up and around and around until her feet knew to stop.

She entered a door, and there she saw nailed up on the wall the document that had been stamped with the gold seal and framed in the gold frame which matched the dream that was hung up in her head.

"Here I be," she said. There was a fixed and ceremonial stiffness over her body.

"A charity case, I suppose," said an attendant who sat at the desk before her.

But Phoenix only looked above her head. There was sweat on her face; the wrinkles shone like a bright net.

"Speak up, Grandma," the woman said. "What's your name? We must have your history, you know. Have you been here before? What seems to be the trouble with you?"

Old Phoenix only gave a twitch to her face as if a fly were bothering her.

"Are you deaf?" cried the attendant.

But then the nurse came in.

"Oh, that's just old Aunt Phoenix," she said. "She doesn't come for herself — she has a little grandson. She makes these trips just as regular as clockwork. She lives away back off the Old Natchez Trace." She bent down. "Well, Aunt Phoenix, why don't you just take a seat? We won't keep you standing after your long trip." She pointed.

The old woman sat down, bolt upright in the chair.

"Now, how is the boy?" asked the nurse.

Old Phoenix did not speak.

"I said, how is the boy?"

But Phoenix only waited and stared straight ahead, her face very solemn and withdrawn into rigidity.

"Is his throat any better?" asked the nurse. "Aunt Phoenix, don't you hear me? Is your grandson's throat any better since the last time you came for the medicine?"

With her hand on her knees, the old woman waited, silent, erect and motionless, just as if she were in armor.

"You mustn't take up our time this way, Aunt Phoenix," the nurse said. "Tell us quickly about your grandson, and get it over. He isn't dead, is he?"

At last there came a flicker and then a flame of comprehension across her face, and she spoke.

"My grandson. It was my memory had left me. There I sat and forgot why I made my long trip."

"Forgot?" The nurse frowned. "After you came so far?"

Then Phoenix was like an old woman begging a dignified forgiveness for waking up frightened in the night. "I never did go to school — I was too old at the Surrender," she said in a soft voice. "I'm an old woman without an education. It was my memory fail me. My little grandson, he is just the same, and I forgot it in the coming."

"Throat never heals, does it?" said the nurse, speaking in a loud, sure voice to Old Phoenix. By now she had a card with something written on it, a little list. "Yes. Swallowed lye. When was it — January — two — three years ago — "

Phoenix spoke unasked now. "No, missy, he not dead, he just the same. Every little while his throat begin to close up again, and he not able to swallow. He not get his breath. He not able to help himself. So the time come around, and I go on another trip for the soothing medicine."

"All right. The doctor said as long as you came to get it you could have it," said the nurse. "But it's an obstinate case."

"My little grandson, he sit up there in the house all wrapped up, waiting by himself," Phoenix went on. "We is the only two left in the world. He suffer and it don't seem to put him back at all. He got a sweet look. He going to last. He wear a little patch quilt and peep out, holding his mouth open like a little bird. I remembers so plain now. I not going to forget him again, no, the whole enduring time. I could tell him from all the others in creation."

"All right." The nurse was trying to hush her now. She brought her a bottle of medicine. "Charity," she said, making a check mark in a book.

Old Phoenix held the bottle close to her eyes and then carefully put it into her pocket.

"I thank you," she said.

"It's Christmas time, Grandma," said the attendant. "Could I give you a few pennies out of my purse?"

"Five pennies is a nickel," said Phoenix stiffly.

"Here's a nickel," said the attendant.

Phoenix rose carefully and held out her hand. She received the nickel and then fished the other nickel out of her pocket and laid it beside the new one. She stared at her palm closely, with her head on one side.

Then she gave a tap with her cane on the floor.

"This is what come to me to do," she said. "I going to the store and buy my child a little windmill they sells, made out of paper. He going to find it hard to believe there such a thing in the world. I'll march myself back where he waiting, holding it straight up in this hand."

She lifted her free hand, gave a little nod, turned round, and walked out of the doctor's office. Then her slow step began on the stairs, going down.

Discussion

1. Do you think you have so intimate a knowledge of your neighborhood as Aunt Phoenix does of hers?
2. How responsive would you say Aunt Phoenix is to all the sense impressions around her? Does her responsiveness (or lack of it) correspond to your own experience of old people?
3. Make a separate list for (a) the visual (sight), (b) the auditory (sound), and (3) the tactile (touch) descriptions. How much of this imagery would you be able to use in a brief description of Aunt Phoenix's return?

FORMAL WRITING   **Describing a Walk through Your Neighborhood**   Your major writing assignment for this chapter will enable you to make use of what you've done up to now — your walk, your list of twenty objects, and the ten sentences or paragraph.

1. Now, you will want to expand that paragraph into a three-paragraph essay, focusing on as much detail as possible. Not only will you be describing what you saw, but you will be quite literally telling a story of your walk. Since nearly all stories have a beginning, a middle, and an end, your three paragraphs will be divided in just that way and in just that order — your first paragraph describing what you saw in the initial phase of your walk; paragraph two will describe you in middle passage, and paragraph three will describe the final phase and conclude the essay.

2. Before you begin writing, get out your list and the paragraph and reread both. Remember, in this essay you are striving for specificity; you want to make each image so clear and sharp that your reader feels able to reach out and touch everything you describe.

3. Once you have completed the essay to your satisfaction, read it through (or have a friend or a family member read it to you), keeping in mind all you've learned about precision and specificity in descriptive writing.

4. To help you get started on your own, read the following account of a neighborhood walk. It, too, began with a list of twenty things observed, which in turn were absorbed into ten sentences. Now, you see those sentences revised, expanded and more richly detailed, organized into an essay.

Pay particular attention to the writer's organization: He begins by leaving his gate and tripping on a beer can and ends returning a friendly growl to a neighbor's dog.

A Saturday's Walk around My Neighborhood

Although I have always lived in a big city, I am generally not aware of it as a fact or what that fact means. But Saturday morning when I left my house for my walk through my neighborhood, even with the first step I took outside my gate, my foot clomped down on a half-flattened beer can, but then when I counted four more before reaching the corner, I began to consider who I was and where I lived. But then I crossed the street, and there leaning against a No Parking sign was an old porcelain kitchen sink, browned by two generations of stains. Next to it was the weathered torso of an ancient Singer sewing machine. I thought that if a person is what he or she eats, then a neighborhood is what it throws away.

I continued up the block, noticing or at least being aware of for the first time, how much of my neighborhood consists of row houses, some built straight up, some protruding with bellylike bay windows. My mother tells my father this is not architectural, but is from too much beer. Reaching the corner of this short block, I looked up at the tall, dark, and brooding St. John's Hospital, which impresses me more as Count Dracula's Home for Aged Vampires. Opposite it and diagonally across from where I stood was a tiny, tree-studded park enclosing a statue of John Hancock. Remembering what he was famous for, I looked to see if he had his quill in his hand, but no, his arms were folded in a posture that suggested, "I dare you." He seemed to be gazing off into the distance, probably into Pauline's Beauty Parlor.

Turning to my right, I advanced slowly up the next block that runs parallel to mine. It, too, consists of brownstone row houses. The attention-getter here was the hulk of a blue 1957 Pontiac that strippers had reduced to a gaping skeleton. But why a copy of *Consumer* on the back seat? I pondered this rounding the corner, again to my right, when, oh! sweet distraction, the heavy wafting smell of oil and flour informed me that Alvarez's Pizza Hut was not far off. Imagining was enough: I bit into one of his crisp, saucy pizza slices, with the melted cheese gripping my upper palate, the hot tomato sauce swooshing against the sides of my mouth like a thick, spicy shower. I let imagination suffice. The noise of the early baseball players caught my attention over in the school ground. Just across from it, facing Alvarez's is the entrance to the park. Elderly residents were out walking their dogs, while alongside the park front, favorite benches were already in occupancy by morning sitters.

On my side of the street, in front of the vacant lot next to Alvarez's, I stopped to admire those beautiful blue flowers (or were they weeds?) growing randomly and profusely. Next to this lot, or rather a part of it, is an old frame house, the only one for blocks around; dark, secluded and shuttered, it sits far back off the street, almost concealed by two gigantic oak trees. I think I've heard it's become a museum or some other kind of city monument. Adjacent to it is one of those big-city apartment buildings. If buildings dream of their past, this one ought never to be reminded of its present.

At this point, I've re-entered the block I live in. The pastor of Zion Church greeted me with a hello as he locked the side door. But already my eye was on Peter, the mangy, toothless mutt that belongs to a family living two doors from me. Peter growled, bared his purple gums and arched his back as if he thought he was a cat. I said, "Hi, Peter." He sniffed, wagged his tail. It was a greeting of return from my trip around my neighborhood.

Checklist for Use before Writing Final Draft

1. Did you organize your paper so that the first paragraph of your description told about the beginning of your walk; the second paragraph focused on the middle of your walk; and the third paragraph described the end of your walk?
2. Have you emphasized the significant details of your walk through the use of accurate and precise words?
3. Have you enriched these details through the use of modifiers and comparisons which enable the readers to sense these details for themselves?
4. Can you locate the subject-verb core in each of your sentences?

Chapter Four

Combining Description and the Anecdote

Have you ever noticed that when you try to describe a new acquaintance to your friends, someone will inevitably ask, But what's she like? As you search for an answer, you think of an event which captures the individual's personality. As you tell about the incident, your listeners' faces reveal their understanding of what you are trying to say. This use of an anecdote, or narrative incident, is a valuable technique often used by writers to clarify their descriptions. It permits them to focus more sharply on key features of their subject. In addition, the dramatic quality of the story strengthens the impact of the description. In this chapter you will continue to develop your skills in description and you will also learn how to construct such anecdotes so that your writing will be more vigorous and your points more clearly made. You will be asked to investigate an important new source of material — your memories, specifically, your past experiences in school. As you focus on particular events, you will discover that colors, shapes, sounds, and even smells are stored in your memory. And most of all you will find that the incidents you remember about people give richness and texture to your recollections.

Since narrative deals with action, you will need to work further on the words that provide movement in your writing. These words, the verbs of the sentence, are often the source of problems for writers, and you will have a chance to deal with the difficulties raised by writing in the past tense.

Writing about a School Experience Below is a "Peanuts" cartoon in which Sally tells one important piece of information she learned at school. With one or two other students in the class, make your own list of important things you learned. Your list may include both academic and also non-academic areas.

When you have finished, compare your list with those of the other groups in the class.

Discussion

1. Were there any items that were on everybody's list?
2. Which items do you think are most important?

In the following article, Russell Baker gives his ideas on the kind of education we acquire in our schools.

When you finish reading the article, see if there are any items that Baker discusses that you might want to add to your list.

© 1975 United Feature Syndicates, Inc.

SCHOOL VS. EDUCATION — Russell Baker

By the age of six the average child will have completed the basic American education and be ready to enter school. If the child has been attentive in these pre-school years, he or she will already have mastered many skills.

From television, the child will have learned how to pick a lock, commit a fairly elaborate bank holdup, prevent wetness all day long, get the laundry twice as white and kill people with a variety of sophisticated armaments.

From watching his parents, the child, in many cases, will already know how to smoke, how much soda to mix with whisky, what kind of language to use when angry and how to violate the speed laws without being caught.

At this stage, the child is ready for the second stage of education which occurs in school. There, a variety of lessons may be learned in the very first days.

The teacher may illustrate the economic importance of belonging to a strong union by closing down the school before the child arrives. Fathers and mothers may demonstrate to the child the social cohesion that can be built on shared hatred by demonstrating their dislike for children whose pigmentation displeases them. In the latter event, the child may receive visual instruction in techniques of stoning buses, cracking skulls with a nightstick and subduing mobs with tear gas. Formal education has begun.

During formal education the child learns that life is for testing. This stage lasts twelve years, a period during which the child learns that success comes from telling testers what they want to hear.

Early in this stage, the child learns that he is either dumb or smart. If the teacher puts intelligent demands upon the child, the child learns he is smart. If the teacher expects little of the child, the child learns he is dumb and soon quits bothering to tell the testers what they want to hear.

At this point, education becomes more subtle. The child taught by school that he is dumb observes that neither he, she, nor any of the many children who are even dumber ever failed to be promoted to the next grade. From this, the child learns that while everybody talks a lot about the virtue of being smart, there is very little incentive to stop being dumb.

What is the point of school, besides attendance? the child wonders. As the end of the first formal stage of education approaches, school answers this question. The point is to equip the child to enter college.

Children who have been taught they are smart have no difficulty. They have been happily telling testers what they want to hear for twelve years. Being artists at telling testers what they want to hear, they are admitted to college joyously, where they promptly learn that they are the hope of America.

Children whose education has been limited to adjusting themselves to their schools' low estimates of them are admitted to less joyous colleges which, in some cases, may teach them to read.

At this stage of education, a fresh question arises for everyone. If the point of lower education was to get into college, what is the point of college? The answer is soon learned. The point of college is to prepare the student — no longer a child now — to get into graduate school. In college, the student learns that it is no longer enough simply to tell the testers what they want to hear. Many are tested for graduate school; few are admitted.

Those excluded may be denied valuable certificates to prosper in medicine, at the bar, in the corporate boardroom. The student learns that the race is to the cunning and often, alas, to the unprincipled.

Thus, the student learns the importance of destroying competitors and emerges richly prepared to play his role in the great simmering melodrama of American life.

Afterwards, the former student's destiny fulfilled, his life rich with oriental carpets, rare porcelain and full bank accounts, he may one day find himself with the leisure and the inclination to open a book with a curious mind, and start to become educated.

Discussion

1. Are your experiences in school in any way like those described by Russell Baker? Explain.
2. While most people would say that teaching students reading, writing, and arithmetic is the primary responsibility of schools, are there any other subjects that you think should be included? For example, do you think art, music, athletics, or health care should be taught? Which ones? Why?
3. If, as the *Peanuts* cartoon and Baker's essay suggest, schools also teach you how to cope with the world, are there any

suggestions you could make to improve this area of learning?

IN-CLASS
WRITING

Recalling the Classroom Your ideas about education have been formed in part by your past experiences. To a large extent, your memories focus on the teachers you have had, but if you think a minute or two, you will realize that the school, the particular room, also played a part in how you feel about what happened.

Do you remember any particular classroom? Your initial reaction may be negative, but if you give yourself a chance, you will be surprised by how much comes back into your mind. Throughout your years in school, you have been in many different rooms. Choose one early classroom where you felt you learned the most. (Remember, even if you weren't learning the traditional subjects, you were learning something.) Describe that room as vividly as you can and explain why you consider it has been an important place in your life.

Writing from memory involves a slightly different process from writing about the world around you. Instead of spending time observing your surroundings, you should now spend a few minutes listening to your own thoughts. Try to recreate your sense impressions of the classroom that you are going to describe —What color were the walls? How were the seats arranged? What books, posters, bulletin boards, chalkboards were there? Where were they? What sounds can you recall? Were there any distinctive smells? Jot down all the ideas as they occur to you. Don't try to be selective at this point; just get down as much as you can.

After you have exhausted your memory, group your thoughts in some way, possibly having separate sections for each of the senses, or by moving about the room from right to left or near to far. Then write up your description. At the end, write another paragraph in which you explain why this classroom was important to you.

ACTIVITY

Ranking a Teacher Your in-class writing dealt with memories of a classroom, but your most vivid memories probably focus on the many teachers you have had — some remembered happily, others recalled with fear or anger. Everyone remembers some good teachers, and everyone has his or her own idea of what makes a good teacher. In this activity, you will have a chance to compare your ideas with those of others.

Characteristics of a Teacher

Rank the following ten statements that describe the behavior of a teacher. Mark what you consider the most important characteristic of a good teacher "1," the next-most-important characteristic "2," etc.

When you have finished, join three other students in your class, compare your rankings with theirs, discuss your differences and see if you can come up with a consensus — a ranking that is agreeable to all members of the group. Put that ranking in the column labelled *Group decision*.

Your rank	Group decision	A good teacher:
_____	_____	understands how students learn
_____	_____	encourages discussion
_____	_____	plays no favorites
_____	_____	never reprimands a student in front of others
_____	_____	is a warm, friendly person
_____	_____	knows how to enforce discipline
_____	_____	knows his or her subject thoroughly
_____	_____	has a good speaking voice
_____	_____	accepts and is tolerant of individual differences
_____	_____	encourages his or her students to think for themselves.

Discussion

1. Why did you rank the characteristics the way you did? What attitude toward learning did it reveal?
2. What attitude toward learning does a person show by ranking the ability to enforce discipline as the most important characteristic? What attitude is revealed by the person who ranks warmth and friendliness above all other categories?
3. When you were working with your small group, how did you resolve the differences among you?

4. Did you change your mind about the order in which you had originally listed the characteristics? Why?
5. Are there other characteristics you can suggest that should be added to the list?

Writing an Anecdote As you have already learned, good description depends on precision and vividness, but often an entirely descriptive passage can seem lifeless no matter how careful you are in choosing words. One way to enliven your descriptions is through telling a short incident that involves your subject. Such incidents not only hold your reader's interest, but they also make the characteristic you describe come alive. They add a sense of drama.

Narrative incidents or anecdotes are rarely more than a few sentences long, but to be effective they should provide certain key information. You need to explain not only what happened, but who the people were, where it happened, when it happened and, if possible, why it happened the way it did. This information, sometimes called "the five W's" (who, what, where, when, why), is essential to any narrative. Below are two examples of narrative anecdotes. As you read them, see if you can find the answers to the five W's in each of them.

THE BIRTH OF BIGGER NO. 1 — Richard Wright

The birth of Bigger Thomas goes back to my childhood, and there was not just one Bigger, but many of them, more than I could count and more than you suspect. But let me start with the first Bigger, whom I shall call Bigger No. 1.

When I was a bareheaded, barefoot kid in Jackson, Mississippi, there was a boy who terrorized me and all of the boys I played with. If we were playing games, he would saunter up and snatch from us our balls, bats, spinning tops, and marbles. We would stand around pouting, sniffling, trying to keep back our tears, begging for our playthings. But Bigger would refuse. We never demanded that he give them back; we were afraid, and Bigger was bad. We had seen him clout boys when he was angry and we did not want to run that risk. We never recovered our toys unless we flattered him and made him feel that he was superior to us. Then, perhaps, if he felt like it, he condescended, threw them at us and then gave each of us a swift kick in the bargain, just to make us feel his utter contempt.

That was the way Bigger No. 1 lived. His life was a continuous challenge to others. At all times he took his way, right or wrong, and those who contradicted him had him to fight. And never was he happier than when he had someone cornered and at his mercy; it seemed that the deepest meaning of his squalid life was in him at such times.

I don't know what the fate of Bigger No. 1 was. His swaggering personality is swallowed up somewhere in the amnesia of my childhood. But I suspect that his end was violent. Anyway, he left a marked impression upon me; maybe it was because I longed secretly to be like him and was afraid. I don't know.

ADOLPH HITLER — *W. D. Bayles*

Particularly noticeable is his inability to cope with unexpected situations, this having been amusingly revealed when he laid the cornerstone of the House of German Art in Munich. On this occasion he was handed a dainty, rococo hammer for delivering the three traditional strokes to the cornerstone, but not realizing the fragility of the rococo, he brought the hammer down with such force that at the very first stroke it broke into bits. Then, instead of waiting for another hammer, Hitler completely lost his composure, blushed, looked wildly about him in the manner of a small boy caught stealing jam, and almost ran from the scene leaving the cornerstone unlaid. His enjoyment of the Berlin Olympic Games was completely spoilt when a fanatical Dutch woman who had achieved a personal presentation suddenly clasped him in two hefty arms and tried to kiss him in plain view of 100,000 spectators. Hitler could not regain his composure or stand the irreverent guffaws of foreign visitors, and left the Stadium.

Discussion

1. What are the answers to the five W's in the selection by Richard Wright? By W. D. Bayles?
2. What characteristic does each of these incidents attempt to illustrate?
3. What details do the authors include that make these individuals more vivid?

Using Verbs When writing anecdotes, or any narrative, the action words, or verbs, provide much of the force of your sentences. A writer may say, *He walked into the room.* Yet this does not give a very clear indication of how the man entered.

It is much more effective if you can find a substitute for *walk*. If you cannot think of an alternate, you can consult a *thesaurus*, a kind of dictionary that lists together words of similar meaning. For example, if you look up the word *walk* in the thesaurus, you will find, among the many words listed, the following suggestions:

walk   amble, saunter, stroll, stride, strut, swagger, prance, stalk, hobble, shamble, shuffle, slough, stagger, reel, stumble, trudge.

These are just *some* of the entries given!

Rewrite the following sentence five times, using another word for *talk* in each one:

The teacher talked to the class.

If you cannot think of good substitutes for *talk*, consult your thesaurus.

How does the difference in verb affect the meaning of the sentence?

Past Tense

In addition to stating the action, verbs also give an indication of *when* an action took place, that is, they tell us whether it is taking place now (present tense), took place at some earlier time (past tense), or will take place in the future (future tense). Within these broad categories there are a number of variations and a full discussion of all verb forms appears in the Appendix. There are a number of difficulties that can arise in the selection and formation of verb tenses, but only the most common will be treated in the main part of this book — the simple past tense will be discussed here, the present tense in the next chapter. If you have further problems, be sure to consult the Appendix.

You can recognize the past tense of most English verbs by noting that they end with either a -d or -ed.

I trade<u>d</u> my old car for a motorcycle.
We talk<u>ed</u> to our coach for two hours.

If you remove the -d or -ed from the verbs in the examples, you will see that the sentences, although clumsy, are in the present tense. When you speak, you rarely pronounce the -d or -ed very clearly, and if your listeners are confused, they can always ask you what you meant. In writing, however, your reader cannot ask any questions, so you have to be particularly careful to include these endings.

The problem is further complicated by the fact that (instead of just adding the -d or -ed) some of the most commonly used verbs in English change completely their form for the past tense. A few examples are listed below:

Present	Past
am, is	was
are	were
begin	began
can	could
dig	dug
get	got
has, have	had
know	knew
make	made
stink	stank
study	studied
take	took

A fuller list of these verbs appears in the Appendix. If you have any difficulties with them, make a special effort to memorize them.

Exercise

Here is a section from Piri Thomas's *Down These Mean Streets*. It was originally written in the past tense, but it has been rewritten in the present. In the blank spaces, fill in the proper form of the past tense of the verbs printed in italics.

When you're a kid, everything has some kind of special meaning. I always *can* _____ find something to do, even if it *is* _____ doing nothing. But going to school *is* _____ something else. School *stinks* _____. I *hate* _____ school and all its teachers. I *hate* _____ the crispy look of the teachers and the draggy-long hours they *take* _____ out of my life from nine to three-thirty. I *dig* _____ being outside no matter what kind of weather. Only chumps *work* _____ and *study* _____.

Every day *begins* _____ with a fight to get me out of bed for school. Momma *plays* _____ the same record over an' over every day: "Piri, get up, it's time to go to school." And I *play* _____ mine: "Aw, Momma, I don't feel so good. I think I got a fever or something."

Always it *ends* _____ up the same old way: I *get* _____ up and go _____ to school. But I *don't* _____ always stay there. Sometimes, I *report* _____ for class, let my teacher see me and then *begin* _____ the game of sneaking out of the room. It *is* _____ like escaping from some kind of prison. I *wait* _____ for the teacher to turn her back, then I *slip* _____ out of my seat and hugging the floor, *crawl* _____ on my belly toward the door. The other kids *know* _____ what I *am* _____ doing; they *are* _____ trying not to burst out laughing. Sometimes a wise guy near me *makes* _____ a noise to bring the teacher's attention my way. When this *happens* _____, I lay still between the row of desks until the teacher *returns* _____ to whatever he or she *has* _____ been doing.

<table>
<tr><td>FORMAL
WRITING</td><td>

Describing a Former Teacher Write a description of a teacher you particularly liked or one you especially hated. Include in your description an anecdote about this teacher that reveals one of the teacher's significant traits or characteristics.

In writing this description, jot down all your ideas as they occur without worrying about the order. Then organize your notes according to a plan, possibly having one section on physical characteristics and another on personality. Remember all you have learned about writing descriptions — and, if necessary, reread the sections of this book that explain this kind of writing.

</td></tr>
</table>

Checklist for Use before Writing Final Draft

1. In your description of a teacher, did you include an anecdote? Was that incident one that revealed a significant characteristic of the teacher?

2. Did the anecdote answer the questions, *Whom* were you talking

about? *Where* did the event happen? *When* did it happen? *What* exactly occurred? *Why* did it happen?

3. In your description of the appearance of the teacher, did you include sense impressions of sight, sound, and any others that might have been applicable?
4. Did you use vivid and precise words to describe the significant details?
5. Have you used interesting modifiers and comparisons?
6. Was your description organized according to a plan?
7. Have you put the *-d* or *-ed* at the end of the past tense verbs that require it, and have you used the proper form of those verbs that change for the past tense?
8. Did each of your sentences have a subject-verb core?

Piece by piece, hour by hour, in Yellowknife and in Sri Lanka, consciously and unconsciously, people are busy living out their lives. In both of these places and indeed, everywhere in the world, each day records a tiny chapter in all our lives, whether it is tediously boring or momentously significant. Imagine, then, one supreme, all-knowing author who has recorded each day, that is, each chapter in the life of every citizen of our world. A child is born and the Scribe begins his book, recording each day and its events as the child grows, matures, reaches old age, and dies. At death, all the chapters are complete; the book is closed and the story ends.

Imagine, too, a supreme, ever-present reader scanning all the daily accounts of all the lives, past and present, in Yellowknife and in Sri Lanka. This reader would know all the stories of all those lives and, thus, in effect, know the stories of Yellowknife and of Sri Lanka from their first moments of human habitation.

So much for fantasy. Like stories, our daydreams are deliriously intriguing, though they generally don't yield us practical results. The point here is to illustrate how all-pervasive stories — narratives — are. We read them, hear them, sing and dance to them, and, most importantly, live them. Let us go one step further and say that all of our experiences, whether we recognize the fact or not, in some way come back to life embedded in a story that is just waiting to be told.

Chapter Five

Writing about
a Personal Experience

This chapter concentrates on how to write a factual narrative; special emphasis is given to recounting personal experience. What sets a personal-experience narrative apart from other factual narrative is that it allows the writer to summon up the full gamut of feeling and emotions that went with the experience.

In addition to knowing how the narrative works and how its form facilitates suspense, a writer retelling personal experience must employ vocabulary that creates color and intensifies feeling. In this chapter, you will discover how you can use the narrative to equally pointed effect when writing an objective report in which feelings and emotions play no part. So you see that knowing how to handle the narrative form is an important part of college writing in general.

The *happening* presented here is designed to focus your attention on action; since action is communicated through verbs, you will be able to see more clearly why using verbs accurately is crucial to good writing. The *Language Learning* section deals specifically with verbs in the present tense. It is important to recognize the pitfalls of writing in the present tense, especially when you are using the third-person–singular form.

ACTIVITY

Staging an Event For the next 10 minutes, some of you will perform the activities listed below and the rest of you will observe. The performers will be enacting historical figures, but the focus of the activity is on *what* is happening, not on *who* is doing it. The performers should lose themselves in what they are doing and the observers yield to the whole spectacle of actions. A word of caution to the spectators: Do not become so engrossed in what is happening that you fail to jot down some of the things you see going on. It is helpful to jot down a few verbs to describe what's happening. The purpose, once again, is to concentrate on what a character is doing rather than on who is doing it. Here are the actions to be performed:

1. You are Jacque Piccard in the bathyscaphe *Trieste* on the floor of the Marianas Trench in the Pacific Ocean, almost 12 000 m. below sea level.
2. You are a French Foreign Legionnaire lost in the Sahara gasping for water.
3. You have just discovered El Dorado and all its gold.
4. You are a blind Moslem beggar shuffling through the bazaars of Casablanca crying "Alms for the Love of Allah."
5. You are sculpting a gigantic statue of Donald Duck. You are almost finished.
6. You are Salome dancing before the head of John the Baptist on a silver platter.
7. You are Nero fiddling while Rome burns.
8. You are Cleopatra frantically searching for the asp with which you intend to kill yourself, but it has wriggled off under a desk.
9. You are Ponce de Leon bathing in the Fountain of Youth.
10. You are Marilyn Bell swimming across Lake Ontario from Youngstown to Toronto, September 8–9, 1954.

Discussion

1. Observers, tell what it was like watching so many strange activities all happening at the same time.
2. Participants, tell what it was like to do these activities while being watched and watching others.
3. Were you able to focus your attention on one activity rather than trying to watch everything at once? Explain.
4. Can you think of similar situations where you try to see a lot of things going on at the same time? A carnival? A hockey, basketball, or football game? A train station? Now, supposing you were with a blind person at one of these places and were trying to describe to him or her everything you saw; how would you order the events?

Recording What Happened For the writing assignment, participants and observers separate and form small groups. The reason for breaking up this way is, naturally enough, that those of you who were spectators (S-group) will be writing from a perspective quite different from that of the participants (P-group).

Each group will produce an essay describing its version of what went on during the event. Before you begin writing, you will most likely need to decide on which or whose point of view seems most representative of what actually happened. The S-groups will have some advantage in having some notes to reinforce their impressions. When all groups have finished writing, you will want to read your accounts. Here are some questions you might want to consider after having listened to the groups read their papers.

Discussion

1. How much did what you hear correspond to what you saw take place?
2. Did the essays written by the P-group differ significantly from those written by the S-group? If they did, explain what the differences are and account for why they occurred.
3. Did any two essays describe exactly the same things?
4. Did you notice any specific organizational patterns the groups used to describe the various happenings? For example, were the actions listed from near to far, from right to left, from the center outward? Would you say the sequence of things listed was chronological or spatial?

Recognizing the Elements of the Narrative The participants in the above activity were engaged in two important features of the narrative — they were portraying character and they were involved in an action. The spectators, on the other hand, saw the characters and the action in terms of setting, meaning at a specific time and place. With setting, character, and action, you have the three primary elements of narrative, whether of an eyewitness account of a two-car collision or an imaginary tale about a child lost in a haunted house. Individual writers may shift emphasis from one element to another, but few will omit any element entirely. Still, there is more to effective narrative writing than manipulating these three basic elements. You will discover this when you sit down to write your personal experience for the in-class writing.

Let's go back for a moment to the event. Although the three basic narrative elements were present in a limited way, three important ones were not: first, there was no observable beginning, middle, or end; second, there was no suspense resulting from the cumulative rise in interest that leads to a climax — the highest point of action; third, there was no resolution. All the actions in the happening were fragmentary; they began nowhere and led nowhere.

Writing about an Experience All of you have had experiences you believe to have been interesting, entertaining, edifying, or instructive. Choose one to write about. Your main objective now is to present your material so that it makes the fullest possible effect. Easy as it may seem at first, unless you organize your ideas, you are not apt to achieve much success. But organizing your material is not overwhelmingly difficult.

Below are some topic suggestions that might reawaken old experiences you may have thought you had completely forgotten:

1. The day I was
   a. in a traffic accident
   b. made a school-crossing guard
   c. named our team's most valuable player
   d. elected class president
   e. in our class play
2. How I learned not to fear
   a. the dark
   b. riding a bicycle
   c. our neighbor's dog
   d. my father's/mother's anger
   e. dancing the hustle
3. I have never since
   a. picked a fight
   b. driven Dad's car
   c. told a lie

There are a few basic steps in structuring your essay that will most assuredly put you on the right track toward achieving your goal of an exciting essay:

1. Find a theme or frame of reference with which to invest your experience:

   Examples: Out of this hair-raising adventure, I discovered the value of having a true friend who would stand by me in an hour of desperate need.

   From this, I recognized the importance of being able to stand alone.

   As the writer you need not always have a lesson or moral for your reader, but you must be able to see how the experience, whether terrifying or joyous, left an indelible imprint on you.

2. Recall the experience in full detail from start to finish, omitting nothing. You may write all this down in a rough draft or merely sketch it in outline form.

3. Now you are in a position to isolate the key events. Make sure you have maintained the proper sequence of the events. Identify beginning, middle and ending.

4. Add detail. Choose those details that will convey your feelings to your reader; enhance the key events; and establish mood, atmosphere, and suspense.

5. Identify the climax of your story and gear all preceding events toward it.

6. The climax resolves the conflict. Find a suitable statement or two with which to close your story.

If you follow these steps, you will increase the likelihood of realizing the full effects of your story. Use your imagination if your own experiences seem to lack sufficient interest. It is all right to make your reader wonder whether your account is fact or fiction.

Using Verbs in the Present Tense In the previous chapter, you learned about the importance of verbs in a sentence, and how they not only describe the action, but the time the action takes place. Careful writers choose verbs that add clarity, pace, and color to their writing. Especially when telling stories in writing, beginning writers often confuse the various tense forms in several common verbs. Many students have difficulty finding the correct form for the present tense. In some languages, the ending of the verb changes with almost every change in subject (the doer of the

action) or noun. In Spanish, for instance, the changes in the verb
to speak — *hablar* — are:

I speak	yo hablo	we speak	nosotros hablamos
you speak	tu hablas	you (plural) speak	ustedes hablan
you (formal) speak	usted habla	they speak	ellos, ellas hablan
he, she, it speaks	el, ella habla		

Similar changes existed hundreds of years ago in English, but
gradually most of them have dropped out. Today English retains
only one such change in the present tense — the one used when
the subject is *he, she, it,* or words that substitute for them, such as
John, the lady, the radio, this, that.

The present tense form in English of *speak* is:

I speak	we speak
you speak	you speak
he, she, it } speaks	they speak

The change we make, as you can see, is adding
an s. If you have difficulty with this form, you will have to learn
to check your writing carefully whenever you are using the
present tense.

Some verbs do not follow the regular rules completely.
One of the most common is the verb *to be.* The present tense is
given below:

I am	we are
you are	you are
he, she, it } is	they are

You can see, however, that *to be* does retain the s ending for *he,*
she, and *it.*

Exercise

The following passage is taken from the prologue,
"Knoxville Summer 1915," of James Agee's prizewinning
novel *A Death in the Family.* Reversing the tense-changing
exercise in the previous chapter, here we've changed the

present to the past. All you have to do is change the verbs in italics from past into the present tense.

On the rough wet grass of the backyard my father and mother *had* _____ spread quilts. We all *lay* _____ there, my mother, my father, my uncle, my aunt, and I too *was* _____ lying there. First we *were* _____ sitting up, then one of us *lay* _____ down, and then we all *lay* _____ down, on our stomachs, or on our sides, or on our backs, and they *had* _____ kept on talking. They *were* _____ not talking much, and the talk *was* _____ quiet, of nothing in particular, of nothing at all in particular, of nothing at all. The stars *were* _____ wide and alive, they *seemed* _____ each like a smile of great sweetness and they *seemed* _____ very near. All my people *were* _____ larger bodies than mine, quiet, with voices gentle and meaningless like the voices of sleeping birds. One *was* _____ an artist, he *was* _____ living at home. One *was* _____ a musician, she *was* _____ living at home. One *was* _____ my mother who *was* _____ good to me. One *was* _____ my father who *was* _____ good to me. By some chance, here they *were*, _____ all on this earth; and who *should* _____ ever tell the sorrow of being on this earth, lying on quilts, on the grass, in a summer evening, among the sounds of the night. May God bless my people, my uncle, my aunt, my mother, my good father, oh, remember them kindly in their time of trouble; and in the hour of their taking away.

After a little I *was* _____ taken in and put to bed. Sleep, soft smiling, *drew* _____ me unto her: and those *received* _____ me, who quietly *treated* _____ me, as one familiar and well-beloved in that home: but *would* _____ not, no, *would* _____ not, not now, not ever: but *would* _____ not ever tell me who I *was* _____.

Probably the most difficult part of writing a narrative is maintaining a correct sequence of tense, which often involves more than the simple past and present forms. In the original version of the passage, the first sentence uses the present perfect form: "On the rough wet grass of the backyard my father and mother *have spread* quilts." *Have spread* is the *present perfect* form; it tells us that the action of spreading the quilt occurred at some unspecified time before the family lies down and the recollection of all that happened unfolds. Similarly, the *past perfect* form indicates that an action was completed *before* another *past* event occurred.

"I *had watered* all the roses before mother came through the gate, tense and excited." In writing, it is important that you know how to use these forms so that you do not confuse your reader with inappropriate verb forms. Finally, and this is equally important, once you have chosen the tense that most easily conveys what you want to say, you must avoid shifts in tense, shifts, that is, from past to present, from present to past. Such shifts in time jar your reader out of the enjoyment and excitement you have set out to achieve in telling your story.

READING

Read the following passage from *A Rumor of War*, by Philip Caputo. When you have finished, look back again at the Agee passage. These texts present two vastly different worlds, yet each conveys a very intense and intimate personal experience. Study these two excerpts to see how the authors have achieved these effects of intimacy and intensity. What other effects do you discover that are important to a personal experience?

PANGEE TRAP — Philip Caputo

By this time I was sweating so heavily I could hardly see. Half blind, I stumbled off the trail, felt the ground give way and suddenly found myself two feet shorter.

I had fallen into a pangee trap. Fortunately, it was an old one. The stakes were loose and rotten and I suffered nothing more than the mocking grin of the marine who helped pull me out.

The platoon moved cautiously into the village. We broke up into teams and started the search, which amounted to a disorganized rummaging through the villagers' belongings. Maybe it was the effect of my grammar-school civics lessons, but I felt uneasy doing this, like a burglar or one of those bullying Redcoats who used to barge into American homes during our Revolution.

But I was not completely convinced these thatch and bamboo shacks were homes; a home had brick or frame walls, windows, a lawn, a TV antenna on the roof.

Most of the huts were empty, but in one we found a young woman nursing an infant whose head was covered with running sores. Widener and I began sifting through bundles of clothes. Two other marines rolled aside a large, rice-filled urn to see if it concealed a tunnel entrance, while a third poked his bayonet through the walls. We had been told that the VC sometimes hid clips of small-arms ammunition in the walls.

The girl just sat and stared and nursed the baby. The absolute indifference in her eyes began to irritate me. I smiled stupidly and made a great show of tidying up the mess before we left.

See, lady, we're not like the French. We're all-American good-guy GI Joes. We'll tear this place apart if we have to, but we'll put everything back in its place. See, that's what I'm doing now. But if she appreciated my chivalry, she did not show that, either.

The search turned up nothing significant. Peterson passed the word to break for lunch and be ready to move in half an hour. Gratefully, the marines shed their packs and flopped down in the shade of the trees.

Christ, I had never felt so exhausted, and yet I had walked only three miles, less than one-tenth the distances I had marched at Quantico. It must have been the heat, the incredible Southeast Asian heat.

"Sure takes the starch out of a man, don't it?" Wild Bill Campbell said, as if he had read my thoughts. "Know what I could use right now? A cold bottle of San Miguel. Used to drink that when I was on barracks duty in the Philippines. Had me a little house on Subic Bay, maid and everything. Little Filipino girl."

"Jesus Christ, knock it off."

"Ice-cold, lieutenant. Ice-cold bottle of San Miguel'd go down real good about now."

Unable to stand any more of this torture, I walked down to the river, dipped my helmet into the current, and poured the water over my throbbing head. On the way back, I saw an example of the paradoxical kindness-and-cruelty that made Vietnam such a peculiar war.

One of our corpsmen was treating the infant with the skin ulcers, daubing salve on the sores while other marines entertained the baby to keep it from crying. At the same time, and only a few yards away, our interpreter, a Vietnamese marine lieutenant, roughly interrogated a woman who had been tending a fire.

The lieutenant was yelling at her and waving a pistol in front of her ravaged face. This went on for several minutes. Then his voice rose to an hysterical pitch, and holding the forty-five by the barrel, he raised his arms as if to pistol-whip her. I think he would have, but Peterson stepped in and stopped him.

"She is VC, Dai-uy," the lieutenant protested, explaining that the stakes which she had been hardening in the fire were anti-helicopter devices. Peterson said, all right, the stakes would be destroyed; but he was not going to preside over the torture of an old woman, Viet Cong or not.

Looking surprised and disappointed, the Vietnamese lieutenant stalked off, warning us that we would learn how things were done around here. The old woman shuffled away, a sack of bones covered by a thin layer of shrivelled flesh. The Enemy.

The company moved out half an hour later.

LANGUAGE LEARNING

Writing Dialogue When you write about an event, one of the best ways to make the experience come alive for your readers is to record what was actually said.

If you look back at "Pangee Trap," you will see how the use of dialogue gave you a sense of actually being on the scene. The author probably did not remember the specific words that were spoken, but by combining his memory with his imagination he was able to recreate what might have been said. When you write about an experience, you too will find that you don't remember the exact language that was used. By using your general impression as a starting point, however, you can probably make up sentences that fit the situation.

If you remember a teacher who was always yelling at the class, but don't remember precisely what he or she said, you might make up a speech like this: "I want quiet in this classroom and I want it NOW!!!" screamed Mr. Simpson.

There is a particular form that all writers use when they include dialogue. This form is useful; it lets the reader know exactly what words were spoken. The rules for the form are quite simple.

1. Quotation marks (",") go *in front of the first word* of the speech you are quoting and *after the last word* of that speech. As long as there is no interruption, it does not matter if the speech is one word or a hundred words in several sentences; you only need quotation marks at the beginning and end of the speech.

> Quoth the Raven, "Nevermore!"

> "We were on the bus when this funny old lady got on. She had four shopping bags and when she tried to get her fare out of her handbag, she dropped one of the shopping bags and all her groceries spilled out," said Jane.

2. The first word of the quotation is capitalized and all end punctuation marks — commas, periods, question marks, exclamation points — are included inside the quotation marks.

> "Didn't you see that stop sign?" asked the cop.

> Mom shouted up the stairs, "You'd better get up now, Jim, or you'll be late."

3. The speaker's manner of talking is usually indicated, but *outside* the quotation marks. Dialogue tags, as we call them, are easy to handle when they come at the beginning or end of the quotation. They are separated from the quotation by a comma.

> "Tomorrow night? I'd love to," said Jane.
> The coach said quietly, "We are going to win."

When the dialogue tag comes in the middle of the quotation, the speech is interrupted. Quotation marks must be used after the last word actually spoken and before the first word of the quote following the tag. Commas, too, must be used to separate the tag from the quote.

> "I rewrote this essay four times," said Mary proudly, "and I finally got an A!"

Remember, these marks can often change the meaning of a sentence. Look at the way the meaning changes in the following example:

> The alligator said Mary ate the frog.
> "The alligator," said Mary, "ate the frog."
> The alligator said, "Mary ate the frog."

Writing about a Personal Experience You should be ready now for your major writing assignment in this chapter. In it you should be able to demonstrate all you have learned about the use of verbs in the last two chapters. And you should be able to fashion a narrative of your own based on an incident from your school years that even today seems particularly important to you. Such an incident may have occurred last week or a dozen years ago, but it should be an event that made a decided impression on you or from which you gained some knowledge about schooling, about other people, and about yourself.

First write a sentence at the top of your page that tells what impression the incident made and what you think you learned. For instance, you might begin by saying, "I'll never forget how embarrassed I was when my first grade teacher. . . ." An opening sentence like this will help you keep your story on a single track. As you write, try to include as much as you can to support your opening statement.

Since this is a first-person–singular account, *I* is the subject of your narrative. Do not let the focus of your account shift from *I* to *you. I* is the one and only subject.

Checklist for Use before Writing Final Draft

1. Have you begun your essay with a sentence that conveys both the impression the incident made on you and what you learned from it?
2. Does your story build naturally on the events as they occurred?
3. Have you given your readers enough information so that they will be able to answer the five W's (who, what, when, where, why)?
4. Have you used modifiers, comparisons, and vivid, precise descriptive details?
5. Have you used dialogue to enrich your story?
6. Have you checked your verbs to see if you omitted the -s ending for third-person verbs in the present tense or the -d or -ed ending in the past tense? Have you used the proper past tense form of any irregular verbs?
7. Did you by mistake switch to *you* instead of *I* as the subject word of your sentences?
8. Do all of your sentences have a subject-verb core?

Chapter Six

Writing a Factual Account

Personal narratives are most exciting when your reader knows how you feel at each step in the action, but there are many times when it is important to tell about an incident as unemotionally and objectively as possible. If you read a newspaper account of an accident, or of the Premier's press conference, you are particularly concerned with precisely what happened rather than with the reporter's feelings about it.

In this chapter we will practise objective reporting.

<u>ACTIVITY</u> **Using Clues to Solve a Mystery** Below is a list of clues for solving a mystery. Form yourselves into groups of four or five students and study the list together. Then see if you can find the murderer, the weapon, the time and place of the murder, and the motive. See if your group can come up with the answers first.

1. Mr. Kelly had a bullet hole in his chest and a knife wound in his back.
2. Mr. Jones shot at an intruder in his apartment building at 12:00 noon.
3. The elevator man saw Mr. Kelly at 12:15 P.M.
4. The bullet in Mr. Kelly's chest matched those in the gun owned by Mr. Jones.
5. Only one bullet had been fired from Mr. Jones's gun.
6. When the elevator man saw Mr. Kelly, Mr. Kelly was bleeding slightly, but he did not seem too badly hurt.

7. A knife with Mr. Kelly's blood on it was found in Miss Smith's yard.
8. The knife in Miss Smith's yard had Mr. Scott's fingerprints on it.
9. Mr. Kelly had destroyed Mr. Jones's business by stealing all his customers.
10. The elevator man saw Mr. Kelly's wife go to Mr. Scott's apartment at 11:30 A.M.
11. The telephone operator said that Mr. Kelly's wife frequently went to Mr. Scott's apartment.
12. Mr. Kelly's body was found in the park.
13. Mr. Kelly's body was found at 1:30 P.M.
14. Mr. Kelly had been dead for 1 hour when his body was found.
15. The elevator man saw Mr. Kelly go to Mr. Scott's room at 12:25 P.M.
16. The elevator man went off duty at 12:30 P.M.
17. Mr. Kelly's body had been dragged a long distance.
18. Miss Smith saw Mr. Kelly go to Mr. Jones' apartment building at 11:55 A.M.
19. Mr. Kelly's wife disappeared after the murder.
20. Mr. Scott disappeared after the murder.
21. Mr. Jones disappeared after the murder.
22. The elevator man said that Miss Smith was in the lobby of the apartment building when he went off duty.
23. Miss Smith often followed Mr. Kelly.
24. Mr. Jones had told Mr. Kelly that he was going to kill him.
25. Miss Smith said that nobody left the apartment building between 12:25 and 12:45 P.M.
26. Mr. Kelly's bloodstains were found in Mr. Scott's car.
27. Mr. Kelly's bloodstains were found in Mr. Jones's car.

Discussion

1. If your group was able to solve the mystery, what factors helped you most?
2. If you could not solve the mystery, what do you think caused the problem?

Establishing Sequence in the Narrative If you were successful in solving the murder mystery, you will have noticed that you had to establish the correct sequence of events in order to find the murderer.

This time sequence, or chronology, along with the five W's (who, where, when, what, why) that you learned about when you wrote anecdotes in Chapter 4, are the basic ingredients in all narratives. In writing a factual report, they are even more valuable since your reader's interest is focused on knowing "What happened first?" and "Then what happened?" and "What happened after that?"

A factual account ought to be as objective as you can make it. Complete objectivity is rarely possible. It is, however, important neither to praise nor to blame, but simply to tell the facts in the order in which they occurred. The writer should avoid all words that excite an emotional response.

IN-CLASS WRITING

Reporting the Murder   Write an account of the events that led up to the murder. Your opening sentence should tell who did it, what he or she did, when and where it occurred, and why. Then going back to the first significant event from among the clues, tell the incidents as they occurred. Be sure to keep the proper time sequence and to be as objective as you can. (If you were not able to solve the mystery, read through this chapter until you find the paragraph in which the answer is buried.)

LANGUAGE LEARNING

Using Pronouns   Mystery stories are fun to read because you know you are supposed to be confused. But sometimes you create mysteries in your writing when you don't intend to. Your readers don't understand what is happening and get annoyed or bored rather than intrigued. One such confusion occurs when you use *he, she,* or *they* and the reader doesn't know which person or persons are meant. Look at the following passage:

> Maria, Joe, James, and Cheryl went to Burger King to buy lunch. *She* wanted a Junior Whopper, but *they* wanted Whoppers. *He* wanted *his* with lettuce and pickles, while *she* wanted *hers* with onion and ketchup. *They,* however, wanted *theirs* with "the works."

Which person got which hamburger? Rewrite the passage and put in names in place of the italicized words. Compare your version with your classmates'. How many different ways were there to distribute the hamburgers?

Words like *he, she,* and *they* — called pronouns — are used to prevent the monotony caused by having to say the name of a person, place, or thing over and over again. The most frequently used forms are usually listed in the following way:

First person (used to substitute for the *speaker*):

Singular	Plural
I	we
my, mine	our, ours
me	us

Second person (used to substitute for the *person being spoken to*):

Singular and plural (the same form is used for both)
you
your, yours
you

Third person (used to substitute for a *person, place, or thing being talked about*):

Singular			Plural		
Masculine	Feminine	Neuter	Masculine	Feminine	Neuter
he	she	it		they	
his	her, hers	its *		their, theirs	
him	her	it		them	
				(the same form is used for all)	

If you were the waiter or waitress at Burger King, you could tell who wanted the hamburgers by watching the faces or gestures.

But when you are reading, you have no such clues. That is why you have to be careful when you use pronouns. As a general rule, a pronoun refers to the last named person or thing.

Exercise

Read the following sentences and rewrite them in as many ways as you can to cover all possible meanings.

1. James gave Bill a book he liked.
2. Mary and JoAnn helped Sue and Carol into their car.

* Notice that *its* does not have an apostrophe. *It's* is used to mean *it is.*

3. Elaine told Nila that she was going to win the game.
4. We decided to hold an election. That caused trouble.

Read the paragraphs below. They sound very peculiar because we have not used any pronouns. In place of *students* in the first sentence, use *John and Mary*. In the remaining sentences, substitute *John, Mary* or the proper pronoun for *the student*. In some cases, you may have to rewrite the whole sentence.

Two students feel very uncomfortable in composition class. One student hates English while the other student likes to read but thinks writing involves some mysterious process.

One student told the other student that the student has nothing to say and the student does not know what the student can write about. The other student said that the student has many ideas but the student's thoughts seem to get confused when the student has to put the words on paper. Both students hope that the teacher will help solve the problems of the students.

Selecting Significant Detail Writing objectively may not seem particularly difficult since all you have to do is list the facts in the proper order and make sure that you include the five W's (who, what, where, when, why). However, when you start planning your writing, you may discover that there are a tremendous number of facts. Indeed, most of the work that you have done in this book so far has been geared to showing you the vast number of facts that lie around you in even the simplest object. But at the same time you have noticed that some facts are more important than others. *The significant detail* is just another way of saying *the significant fact*.

To write objectively, the crucial step is to decide which facts are significant — which facts need to be emphasized, which facts must be included, and even which facts can be successfully ignored. When you wrote up the murder, you were certainly aware that the crucial facts were that Mr. Scott killed Mr. Kelly. The fact that the murder took place at 12:30 is important to include because it lets your reader know the when and where of the event. At the same time, it probably is not necessary to include the information about a gun.

Look back over the clues of the mystery. Make a list of all those which are *not* significant in solving the crime.

In the mystery story below, the author was very careful to select the details that conveyed the information, and only the information he wanted.

As you read, notice what facts are included.

AUGUST HEAT — William Fryer Harvey

Phenistone Road, Clapham
August 20th, 190-

I have had what I believe to be the most remarkable day in my life, and while the events are still fresh in my mind, I wish to put them down on paper as clearly as possible.

Let me say at the outset that my name is James Clarence Withencroft.

I am forty years old, in perfect health, never having known a day's illness.

By profession I am an artist, not a very successful one, but I earn enough money by my black-and-white work to satisfy my necessary wants.

My only near relative, a sister, died five years ago, so that I am independent.

I breakfasted this morning at nine, and after glancing through the morning paper I lighted my pipe and proceeded to let my mind wander in the hope that I might chance upon some subject for my pencil.

The room, though door and windows were open, was oppressively hot, and I had just made up my mind that the coolest and most comfortable place in the neighbourhood would be the deep end of the public swimming bath, when the idea came.

I began to draw. So intent was I on my work that I left my lunch untouched, only stopping work when the clock of St. Jude's struck four.

The final result, for a hurried sketch, was, I felt sure, the best thing I had done.

It showed a criminal in the dock immediately after the judge had pronounced sentence. The man was fat — enormously fat. The flesh hung in rolls about his chin; it creased his huge, stumpy neck. He was clean shaven (perhaps I should say a few days before he must have been clean shaven) and almost bald. He stood in the dock, his short, clumsy fingers clasping the rail, looking straight in front of him. The feeling that his expression conveyed was not so much one of horror as of utter, absolute collapse.

There seemed nothing in the man strong enough to sustain that mountain of flesh.

I rolled up the sketch, and without quite knowing why, placed it in my pocket. Then with the rare sense of happiness which the knowledge of a good thing well done gives, I left the house.

I believe that I set out with the idea of calling upon Trenton, for I remember walking along Lytton Street and turning to the right along Gilchrist Road at the bottom of the hill where the men were at work on the new train lines.

From there onwards I have only the vaguest recollection of where I went. The one thing of which I was fully conscious was the awful heat, that came up from the dusty asphalt pavement as an almost palpable wave. I longed for the thunder promised by the great banks of copper-coloured cloud that hung low over the western sky.

I must have walked five or six miles, when a small boy roused me from my reverie by asking the time.

It was twenty minutes to seven.

When he left me I began to take stock of my bearings. I found myself standing before a gate that led into a yard bordered by a strip of thirsty earth, where there were flowers, purple stock and scarlet geranium. Above the entrance was a board with the inscription —

CHS. ATKINSON   MONUMENTAL MASON
WORKER IN ENGLISH AND ITALIAN MARBLES

From the yard itself came a cherry whistle, the noise of hammer blows, and the cold sound of steel meeting stone.

A man was sitting with his back towards me, busy at work on a slab of curiously veined marble. He turned round as he heard my steps and I stopped short.

It was the man I had been drawing, whose portrait lay in my pocket.

He sat there, huge and elephantine, the sweat pouring from his scalp, which he wiped with a red silk handkerchief.

But though the face was the same, the expression was absolutely different.

He greeted me smiling, as if we were old friends, and shook my hand.

I apologised for my intrusion.

"Everything is hot and glary outside," I said. "This seems an oasis in the wilderness."

"I don't know about the oasis," he replied, "but it certainly is hot, as hot as hell. Take a seat, sir!"

He pointed to the end of the gravestone on which he was at work, and I sat down.

"That's a beautiful piece of stone you've got hold of," I said.

He shook his head. "In a way it is," he answered; "the surface here is as fine as anything you could wish, but there's a big flaw at the back, though I don't expect you'd ever notice it. I could never make really a good job of a bit of marble like that. It would be all right in the summer like this; it wouldn't mind the blasted heat. But wait till the winter comes. There's nothing quite like frost to find out the weak points in stone."

"Then what's it for?" I asked.

The man burst out laughing.

"You'd hardly believe me if I was to tell you it's for an exhibition, but it's the truth. Artists have exhibitions; so do grocers and butchers; we have them too. All the latest little things in headstones, you know."

He went on to talk of marbles, which sort best withstood wind and rain, and which were easiest to work; then of his garden and a new sort of carnation he had bought. At the end of every other minute he would drop his tools, wipe his shining head, and curse the heat.

I said little, for I felt uneasy. There was something unnatural, uncanny, in meeting this man.

I tried at first to persuade myself that I had seen him before, that his face, unknown to me, had found a place in some out-of-the-way corner of my memory, but I knew that I was practising little more than a plausible piece of self-deception.

Mr. Atkinson finished his work, spat on the ground, and got up with a sign of relief.

"There! what do you think of that?" he said, with an air of evident pride.

The inscription which I read for the first time was this —

SACRED TO THE MEMORY
OF
JAMES CLARENCE WITHENCROFT
BORN JAN. 18th, 1860
HE PASSED AWAY VERY SUDDENLY
ON AUGUST 20TH, 190-

"In the midst of life we are in death."
For some time I sat in silence. Then a cold shudder ran down my spine. I asked him where he had seen the name.

"Oh, I didn't see it anywhere," replied Mr. Atkinson. "I wanted some name, and I put down the first that came into my head. Why do you want to know?"

"It's a strange coincidence, but it happens to be mine."

He gave a long, low whistle.

"And the dates?"

"I can only answer for one of them, and that's correct."

"It's a rum go!" he said.

But he knew less than I did. I told him of my morning's work. I took the sketch from my pocket and showed it to him. As he looked, the expression of his face altered until it became more and more like that of the man I had drawn.

"And it was only the day before yesterday," he said, "that I told Maria there were no such things as ghosts!"

Neither of us had seen a ghost, but I knew what he meant.

"You probably heard my name," I said.

"And you must have seen me somewhere and have forgotten it! Were you at Clacton-on-Sea last July?"

I had never been to Clacton in my life. We were silent for some time. We were both looking at the same thing, the two dates on the gravestone, and one was right.

"Come inside and have some supper," said Mr. Atkinson.

His wife was a cheerful little woman, with the flaky red cheeks of the country-bred. Her husband introduced me as a friend of his who was an artist. The result was unfortunate, for after the sardines and watercress had been removed, she brought out a Dore Bible, and I had to sit and express my admiration for nearly half an hour.

I went outside, and found Atkinson sitting on the gravestone smoking.

We resumed the conversation at the point we had left off.

"You must excuse my asking," I said, "but do you know

of any thing you've done for which you could be put on trial?"

He shook his head.

"I'm not a bankrupt, the business is prosperous enough. Three years ago I gave turkeys to some of the guardians at Christmas, but that's all I can think of. And they were small ones, too," he added as an afterthought.

He got up, fetched a can from the porch, and began to water the flowers. "Twice a day regular in the hot weather," he said, "and then the heat sometimes gets the better of the delicate ones. And ferns, good Lord! They could never stand it. Where do you live?"

I told him my address. It would take an hour's quick walk to get back home.

"It's like this," he said. "We'll look at the matter straight. If you go back home to-night, you take your chance of accidents. A cart may run over you, and there's always banana skins and orange peel, to say nothing of fallen ladders."

He spoke of the improbable with an intense seriousness that would have been laughable six hours before. But I did not laugh.

"The best thing we can do," he continued, "is for you to stay here till twelve o'clock. We'll go upstairs and smoke; it may be cooler inside."

To my surprise I agreed.

We are sitting now in a long, low room beneath the eaves. Atkinson has sent his wife to bed. He himself is busy sharpening some tools at a little oilstone, smoking one of my cigars the while.

The air seems charged with thunder. I am writing this at a shaky table before the open window. The leg is cracked, and Atkinson, who seems a handy man with his tools, is going to mend it as soon as he has finished putting an edge on his chisel.

It is after eleven now. I shall be gone in less than an hour.

But the heat is stifling.

It is enough to send a man mad.

Discussion

1. What facts did the author emphasize?
2. What was the effect of his constant mention of the heat?

Observing a School Scene   Go to some place in your school where students congregate — their home room, the cafeteria, the gym, or one of the lawns. Position yourself some place where you can survey the scene and watch closely for at least 20 minutes. You will need to have paper and pencil with you. Without focusing on anything in particular, just jot down what you see and hear. Don't try to be selective at this point, but do check to see that you have material to answer the five W's (who, what, where, when, why).

When you have finished your observation, sit some place that is quiet and look over all the facts you have collected. Is there any one impression (fact) that stands out? Has your observation shown that the students in your school on a sunny day in May are lazy and spend a lot of time sitting idly on the grass? Or is it that on cold days in February, students in the cafeteria stick together in small, unfriendly cliques? Has the spring weather brought out a sudden spurt in athletic activities? It is vital to your paper that you find one central impression to emphasize; don't write until you have discovered it.

Finding the dominant impression may seem to be a difficult task, but there are certain approaches that will make it easier. You could, for instance, count the number of examples you have of people moving and compare the total with the number of people sitting or standing still; or you could add up the number of people who are alone and contrast it with the number of people in groups. Another approach is to try to remember what incident or scene struck you most forcibly; it might have been a Frisbee game or two students having a strenuous argument. More than anything else, the dominant impression is your perception of the scene. It does not have to be the same as anyone else's, and the only requirement is that your details support your impression.

Once you have found the impression you wish to emphasize, go over your notes and find all the other facts that fit with this one. You may recall something not in the notes. You will want your paper to have a sense of all its parts fitting together, so you must be careful to include all the material that belongs. At this point, too, you will want to make sure you have given the details of where, when, what, and why — as well as who. You may have some facts that do not fit at all. These will have to be discarded. As you write, check the words you use to make sure you are neither praising or blaming and that you have avoided words with strong emotional charge.

An objective narrative can be very dull if it is only a collection of unrelated facts — you and your reader will find this objective narrative interesting if it is centered around a significant impression about the people and the place you chose.

Checklist for Use before Writing Final Draft:

1. Can you identify impressions you wished to emphasize?
2. Does the information in your paper support the dominant impressions?
3. Do you have the information to answer who, what, where, when, and, if possible, why?
4. Have you used precise words, interesting modifiers and comparisons?
5. When you use pronouns, is it clear to whom or to what you are referring?
6. Do you have the -s ending on present-tense verbs with *he, she,* or *it?*
7. Have you used the proper past-tense forms?

Chapter Seven

Putting Emotion
in the Narrative

In this chapter, you will discover ways to create mood and atmosphere that heighten the excitement of your story. To communicate the genuine feelings that help deepen your story's meaning and importance, it is important to resist the temptation to *tell* your readers exactly what they should feel. Instead, expose them directly to the pain, the joy, the fear, and the terror your words and images have created. When their hands shake in terror, when their eyes light up, when sweat trickles down their backs, you — as a writer — have succeeded in doing exactly what you set out to do.

As you work to make your readers feel what you want them to feel, you must, however, make sure that you are writing correct and complete sentences. Sentences that are vaguely worded, awkwardly constructed, or incomplete confuse your readers and make them lose interest.

ACTIVITY **Writing Plays and Stories from Pictures** On pp. 86–89, you will find a group of pictures. Each one shows two people engaged in some activity. As you look at the pictures, try to imagine what events might have led up to the scene. For instance, what has led up to the fight between the two children? What brought the old couple together at the senior citizens' dance?

Now assemble into groups of four or five, choose one of the pictures and work together to decide on one explanation of it.

Together create the outlines of a short play or story that will dramatize the events. If you decide to write a play, it is not necessary to write the dialogue exactly, but you should have a few scenes and a clear idea of what will happen in each of them. Decide who will play each role and approximately what each character will say. If you decide to write a story, include some conversation between the characters in the picture.

When all the groups are ready, present your play, or read your story to the rest of the class. Some of you may feel shy about acting or reading, but remember you are not expected to be professionals; you are simply presenting your ideas in one of the pleasantest forms of communication.

Discussion

1. Name and discuss those emotions the plays and short stories dealt with.
2. Considering the characters and situations the writers created, do you think the emotions portrayed were appropriate and consistent? Cite examples.
3. Did any of the authors give sufficient attention to mood and atmosphere? Cite examples.
4. As writers, explain the difficulties you encountered in communicating emotion in plays and stories.

LANGUAGE LEARNING

Choosing the Right Word You have been learning the importance of choosing the right word to make your description and narrative more effective and vivid. Choosing the right word heightens any kind of dramatic writing because it enables your readers to visualize the action and at the same time respond to the emotions the characters feel.

However, it is important for you to decide what emotion or emotions of the characters you want to convey. For instance, if you were telling of your first date, what were the emotions you felt? Did you feel nervous, excited, deliriously happy, apprehensive? Or on your first day in high school, were you anxious, scared, worried? In the same way, try to imagine the feelings of the characters in your play or story and see if you can convey these feelings through their words and actions.

Below is a description of an ordinary daily activity deliberately exaggerated to create the feeling that an ominous, frightening calamity is about to engulf the narrator. As you read, give special attention to the words that generate and sustain the emotional effect intended — fear:

> With great deliberation, I pushed open the door; it closed behind me with a dull, morose thud. I strode boldly toward the gleaming white box, ignoring the heavy thumping of my heart and the quick gasps of my breathing. My hand reached out for the handle. My icy fingers were as chilly as the metal handle. The door of the box opened soundlessly as I pulled. Slowly, carefully, I put my hand into that vast open space. I gasped as my fingers met a soft, slimy mass. I felt a smooth, glassy surface. Jerking away, I hit against a rough, prickly thing that scratched the back of my hand. Suddenly I felt a waxy rectangle. "The milk container, at last," I muttered to myself. "Tomorrow I'll have to have the light in the refrigerator fixed."

The *I* in the passage above is doing a very ordinary thing — opening a refrigerator — something we all do several times a day. For most of us, our daily lives consist for the most part of doing very routine, but very necessary activities, such as catching a bus — and maybe missing it; fixing a sandwich or a flat tire; selecting the right sweater or pair of slacks to wear to school. For most of us — fortunately, no doubt — momentous events occur infrequently.

On the other hand, TV series like *All in the Family, Three's Company,* and *The Jeffersons* owe their popularity to their weekly portrayals of disaster, calamity, and misfortune that befall, but never conquer very ordinary people. What accounts for the success of these shows is the ability of their scriptwriters to convince us that, in spite of the weekly traumas they suffer, Archie and Edith, George and Louise, and Chrissy, Janet and Jack are really just like us.

IN-CLASS WRITING   **Writing an Episode for a TV Show**   This is an individual writing assignment in which you are asked to choose any character or group of characters from your favorite TV show and write a brief episode of your own imagining. You may present your characters in a familiarly typical setting, for example: Sanford, of *San-*

ford & Son hiding from Lamont the truth of something he's done and doesn't want revealed; Baretta on the chase of a thief and murderer; Archie berating Edith for doing a kind deed. Or, you may conceive of these characters in a totally different setting, presenting a totally different set of responses. You may see Archie, heroic and self-sacrificing, lost and alone at the North Pole. You might see Edith as a glamorous femme fatale, the female counterpart of James Bond.

However you imagine the situation and your characters, try to create a mood and atmosphere that sets the stage for what is to happen. Engage the character in an action where a dominant emotion is expressed. You may write your sketch as either a short story or a play.

Writing Complete Sentences In the previous assignment, you probably discovered, if you were writing a story, that you needed to express most of your ideas in complete sentences. On the other hand, if you were writing a play, you most likely found that in writing your dialogue you did not need to write complete sentences. As you have no doubt observed in your own conversations with your friends, people rarely talk to each other in complete sentences. Sometimes they are interrupted by someone else, and sometimes they just don't finish the sentence because the conclusion is obvious from their facial expression or their gestures.

Another discovery you probably made in doing this assignment is that in writing all of your meaning, all of the feeling and emotion you wanted to convey had to be communicated in words on a page. Because it was not spoken language, you did not have tone of voice, facial expressions, and gestures to fill out the idea you were communicating; you had to find the right word and fit it into a meaningful sentence. Whatever the number of readers you were writing for, not one would be in your presence to ask, "Would you repeat that?" or to say, "I'm not sure I know what you're driving at."

Because you have far more experience talking than writing, you probably tend to transfer the way you speak to the way you write. And because you so frequently converse in incomplete sentences, you may find yourself writing them without realizing they are not complete. The reason for this is simple; it is in the very nature of the difference between speech and writing. Your conversa-

tions in the cafeteria, on the telephone, at your friends' houses —
all of these are simply a series of chain reactions of questions and
replies, exclamations, and pauses between you and the person
you're talking to.

Once the chain reactions are set in motion, there is no further
need either to ask or reply in complete sentences. It is important
to keep in mind here that questions are sentences too, but instead
of giving information or opinions, they ask for it. Look, now, at
the brief dialogue below that attempts to capture the kinds of sentences and non-sentences we use in our daily speech:

Joe   See that girl over there?
Pete   Which one?
Joe   Talking to James.
Pete   Yeah?
Joe   She used to go around with my brother.
Pete   When?
Joe   In high school. But they broke up after a couple of months.
Pete   Why?
Joe   Because she always wanted him to take her out to expensive
        places. And . . . well, he got tired. You know . . . always
        shelling out. So. Well, you know what I mean. . . .
Pete   Yeah, sure. Well, have to go now. See you later.

Now look at the same scene rendered according to the demands of Standard Written English:

> Pete and Joe were sitting in the Royal Café on Mon-
> day having a Coke when an attractive girl walked in. She was
> accompanied by a friend of Pete and Joe, a fellow named
> James. Joe pointed her out to Pete, telling him that when she
> and his brother, Hal, were in high school, they had dated
> steadily. He continued to say that they finally broke up. Hal
> complained that he was always spending money on her, tak-
> ing her to expensive places. Joe's voice trailed off without
> ever quite finishing his sentence. Pete, though, seemed to un-
> derstand what Joe was getting at. Anyway, by that time, Pete
> had to go to class.

The difference between speech and writing may be getting
clearer to you now. As you see, writing requires an individual and
sustained effort in communication. Not only that, but each part of
the communication has to be complete in itself and logically related to the next piece before all the pieces emerge into the whole

message. In other words, written language depends almost exclusively on complete sentences for its meaning. Sentences must be fitted logically to form a further unit of thought called the paragraph. In our example, the second rendition is in the form of a paragraph, but what about the first; would you say Pete and Joe were thinking and talking in a paragraph? We have raised the question only to alert you to the fact that writing is a quite formal activity, much more so than speech.

Exercise

Before returning to the dialogue, you may want to take a brief refresher of the elements of the sentence in Chapter 3. Keep in mind, though, that questions require helping verbs as well as a main verb. Rewrite the dialogue, substituting complete sentences wherever you find an incomplete sentence. Underline the parts that were missing in the original version.

READING

The story below is about a very ordinary man doing something very ordinary, something he has been doing every day for several years — taking a walk. As you read it, try to pinpoint what kind of feeling you are getting, and see if you can discover what the writer has done to evoke this feeling in you.

THE PEDESTRIAN — Ray Bradbury

To enter out into that silence that was the city at eight o'clock of a misty evening in November, to put your feet upon that buckling concrete walk, to step over grassy seams and make your way, hands in pockets, through the silences, that was what Mr. Leonard Mead most dearly loved to do. He would stand upon the corner of an intersection and peer down long moonlit avenues of sidewalk in four directions, deciding which way to go, but it really made no difference; he was alone in this world of A.D. 2131, or as good as alone, and with a final decision made, a path selected, he would stride off sending patterns of frosty air before him like the smoke of a cigar.

Sometimes he would walk for hours and miles and return only at midnight to his house. And on his way he would see the cottages and homes with their dark windows, and it was not unequal to walking through a graveyard, because only the faintest glimmers of firefly light appeared in flickers behind the windows. Sudden gray phantoms seemed to manifest themselves upon inner room walls where a curtain was still undrawn against the night, or there were whisperings and murmurs where a window in a tomblike building was still open.

Mr. Leonard Mead would pause, cock his head, listen, look, and march on, his feet making no noise on the lumpy walk. For a long while now the sidewalks had been vanishing under flowers and grass. In ten years of walking by night or day, for thousands of miles, he had never met another person walking, not one in all that time.

He now wore sneakers when strolling at night, because the dogs in intermittent squads would parallel his journey with barkings if he wore hard heels, and lights might click on and faces appear, and an entire street be startled by the passing of a lone figure, himself, in the early November evening.

On this particular evening he began his journey in a westerly direction, toward the hidden sea. There was a good crystal frost in the air; it cut the nose going in and made the lungs blaze like a Christmas tree inside; you could feel the cold light going on and off, all the branches filled with invisible snow. He listened to the faint push of his soft shoes through autumn leaves with satisfaction, and whistled a cold quiet whistle between his teeth, occasionally picking up a leaf as he passed, examining its skeletal pattern in the infrequent lamplights as he went on, smelling its rusty smell.

"Hello, in there," he whispered to every house on every side as he moved. "What's up tonight on Channel 4, Channel 7, Channel 9? Where are the cowboys rushing, and do I see the United States Cavalry over the next hill to the rescue?"

The street was silent and long and empty, with only his shadow moving like the shadow of a hawk in mid-country. If he closed his eyes and stood very still, frozen, he imagined himself upon the center of a plain, a wintry windless Arizona country with no house in a thousand miles, and only dry riverbeds, the streets, for company.

"What is it now?" he asked the houses, noticing his wrist watch. "Eight-thirty P.M. Time for a dozen assorted murders? A quiz? A revue? A comedian falling off the stage?"

Was that a murmur of laughter from within a moon-white house? He hesitated, but went on when nothing more happened. He stumbled over a particularly uneven section of walk as he came to a cloverleaf intersection which stood silent where two main highways crossed the town. During the day it was a thunderous surge of cars, the gas stations open, a great insect rustling and ceaseless jockeying for position as the scarab beetles, a faint incense puttering from their exhausts, skimmed homeward to the far horizons. But now these highways too were like streams in a dry season, all stone and bed and moon radiance.

He turned back on a side street, circling around toward his home. He was within a block of his destination when the lone car turned a corner quite suddenly and flashed a fierce white cone of light upon him. He stood entranced, not unlike a night moth, stunned by the illumination and then drawn toward it.

A metallic voice called to him:

"Stand still. Stay where you are! Don't move!"

He halted.

"Put up your hands."

"But — " he said.

"Your hands up! Or we'll shoot!"

The police, of course, but what a rare, incredible thing; in a city of three million, there was only one police car left. Ever since a year ago, 2130, the election year, the force had been cut down from three cars to one. Crime was ebbing; there was no need now for the police, save for this one lone car wandering and wandering the empty streets.

"Your name?" said the police car in a metallic whisper. He couldn't see the men in it for the bright light in his eyes.

"Leonard Mead," he said.

"Speak up!"

"Leonard Mead!"

"Business or profession?"

"I guess you'd call me a writer."

"No profession," said the police car, as if talking to itself. The light held him fixed like a museum specimen, needle thrust through chest.

"You might say that," said Mr. Mead. He hadn't written in years. Magazines and books didn't sell any more. Everything went on in the tomblike houses at night now, he thought, continuing his fancy. The tombs, ill-lit by television light, where the people sat like the dead, the gray or multicolored lights touching their expressionless faces but never really touching *them.*

"No profession," said the phonograph voice, hissing. "What are you doing out?"

"Walking," said Leonard Mead.

"Walking!"

"Just walking," he said, simply, but his face felt cold.

"Walking, just walking, walking?"

"Yes, sir."

"Walking where? For what?"

"Walking for air. Walking to *see.*"

"Your address!"

"Eleven South St. James Street."

"And there is air *in* your house, you have an air-*condi-tioner,* Mr. Mead?"

"Yes."

"And you have a viewing screen in your house to see with?"

"No."

"No?" There was a crackling quiet that in itself was an accusation.

"Are you married, Mr. Mead?"

"No."

"Not married," said the police voice behind the fiery beam. The moon was high and clear among the stars and the houses were gray and silent.

"Nobody wanted me," said Leonard Mead, with a smile.

"Don't speak unless you're spoken to!"

Leonard Mead waited in the cold night.

"Just walking, Mr. Mead?"

"Yes."

"But you haven't explained for what purpose."

"I explained: for air and to see, and just to walk."

"Have you done this often?"

"Every night for years."

The police car sat in the center of the street with its radio throat faintly humming.

"Well, Mr. Mead," it said.

"Is that all?" he asked politely.

"Yes," said the voice. "Here." There was a sigh, a pop. The back door of the police car sprang wide. "Get in."

"Wait a minute, I haven't done anything!"

"Get in."

"I protest!"

"Mr. Mead."

He walked like a man suddenly drunk. As he passed the front window of the car he looked in. As he had expected, there was no one in the front seat, no one in the car at all.

"Get in."

He put his hand to the door and peered into the back seat, which was a little cell, a little black jail with bars. It smelled of riveted steel. It smelled of harsh antiseptic; it smelled too clean and hard and metallic. There was nothing soft there.

"Now if you had a wife to give you an alibi," said the iron voice. "But — "

"Where are you taking me?"

The car hesitated, or rather gave a faint whirring click, as if information, somewhere, was dropping card by punch-slotted card under electric eyes. "To the Psychiatric Center for Research on Regressive Tendencies."

He got in. The door shut with a soft thud. The police car rolled through the night avenues, flashing its dim lights ahead.

They passed one house on one street a moment later, one house in an entire city of houses that were dark, but this one particular house had all its electric lights brightly lit, every window a loud yellow illumination, square and warm in the cool darkness.

"That's my house," said Leonard Mead.

No one answered him.

The car moved down the empty river bed streets and off away, leaving the empty streets with the empty sidewalks, and no sound and no motion all the rest of the chill November night.

Discussion

As indicated, the story is about a very ordinary incident, but it does have an unusual end. Even before Mr. Leonard Mead is unexpectedly apprehended by the police car, there is a sense of imminent danger, an atmosphere of fear, that the writer creates.

1. What devices does the writer use to create this feeling?
2. What are some of the "significant details" the writer has used to create the atmosphere?

3. What words has he used to make you aware that something unusual is about to happen?
4. Underline the subject (single line) and verb (double line) of the sentences in paragraphs 2 and 3 of the story. Check with your classmates if you have all underlined the same words.

FORMAL
WRITING

Dramatizing an Ordinary Incident As you have already seen, in a story, the writer should not tell us directly what emotions to feel. We cannot be told to feel apprehensive for Mr. Mead, who certainly does not seem to be afraid at all. But a mood is created so that we, the readers, do feel a certain anxiety.

Write about a very ordinary incident in your life, such as getting up in the morning or travelling to school.

As you did with the personal experience you wrote about in Chapter 5, you will have to organize your ideas. First you need to decide what emotion you want to emphasize. Then you will have to list all phases of the activity to be sure you do not leave anything out. After you have decided which parts you want to be the beginning, middle, and end, think about the kinds of words you can use to make your writing tingle with drama and excitement. If you want to make the incident seem scary, think of all the words that will bring a sense of dread. Some of the words from the paragraph on p. 91 or the story on pp. 94–98 may help you. Whatever your decison is, try to choose your words carefully so that the emotion you want to surround it with becomes clear to the reader. Make sure that the details of the incident also help to reinforce the same emotion.

Checklist for Use before Writing Final Draft

1. Did you use vivid and clear words to describe the people, places, and things in your story?
2. Did you choose the important details to make the drama of your experience more effective?
3. Are your verbs and their forms both correct and dramatic?
4. Are the pronouns you used for your characters clear?
5. Do all your sentences have a subject and verb?
6. Did you have fun writing this story? If you did, so will your readers when they read it!

Chapter Eight

Writing with a Point of View

Sometimes when we retell an event, we find that we are so involved with one person's side of the story that we fail to see any good reason the opposition might have had. Most arguments develop because the persons involved all believe their own position is the right one. When parents and teenagers disagree about the proper time to come home from a party they each have ideas that they think are basic. The parent is worried about the health and welfare of the young person while the teenager is concerned with staying with friends. Each is seeing the problem in a different way, emphasizing different aspects of the issue. We call this difference in seeing a difference in point of view. It is easy to understand how our outward physical position influences our seeing. It is very obvious that a person viewing a city from an airplane will have a different point of view from the person who is walking down a street. But we are not always aware that our inward attitudes also play a decisive part in how we view a situation. These attitudes depend in part on the way we see ourselves. Of course, we don't always see ourselves in exactly the same way all the time. A person may react as a parent in one situation, as a spouse in another, as a professional in a third, or as an American in a fourth. Each of us has a surprising number of ways of seeing ourselves.

ACTIVITY   **Categorizing Yourself** Below is a list of categories in which we often place people. Put a check next to all of the items that fit you. You may add other categories to which you feel you also belong:

teenager	_____
athlete	_____
musician	_____
artist	_____
son	_____
daughter	_____
aunt	_____
uncle	_____
brother	_____
sister	_____
husband	_____
wife	_____
girlfriend	_____
boyfriend	_____
man	_____
woman	_____
worker	_____
Jew	_____
Christian	_____
Moslem	_____
atheist	_____
black	_____
white	_____
Native Indian	_____
Buddhist	_____
Italian	_____
Canadian	_____

Most of us find that we fit into several categories, and we should be aware that our view of a particular situation depends on how we see ourselves at that moment. Yet, even while we share some of the responses of other members of a category, we also know that we are unique individuals who will always be somewhat different from the other members of the group. A basketball player may join with teammates to protest a cut in funds for school athletics, but for reasons that may not be exactly the same as theirs. There are, however, people who do not make this distinction. They see all members of a category as if they were all exactly alike. They may say that athletes are all muscle and no brains or that teenagers are irresponsible and immature. If you are an athlete or a teenager, you know very well that such statements never tell the full truth about you. As an athlete, you know that you have some physical skills, but that is only one part of you; as a teenager, you realize that you may not be grown up in some ways, but that there are many areas in which you are fully mature.

These oversimplified ways of seeing people are called *stereotypes*. The effect of stereotyping an individual can be simply annoying. But stereotyping also causes serious problems when whole groups of people are labelled as if they were all alike, especially, as is often the case, when the description of the group is disparaging and is based on very limited and usually erroneous information. When a person who is not black or not Jewish treats all blacks or Jews as if they were exactly alike, particularly if the generally held view of blacks and Jews is that they are inferior, then he or she has denied them their uniqueness as human beings and their rights as members of society.

The two aspects of point of view that are raised here — how we see ourselves and how we see others — have serious implications for all the writing you do in school. In planning to write narratives, you should understand how these problems affect the presentation of conflicts and thus begin to broaden your range of understanding.

Discussion

1. Look at the list of categories on p. 101. What issues can you think of that would cause differing points of view between a man and a woman? Between an athlete and an artist?
2. What situations can you think of in which people might find a conflict within themselves, such as when a woman is forced to choose between seeing herself as a wife and as a mother?
3. What situations can you think of where conflicts between individuals have become serious because each regarded the other only as a member of a group and not as a unique individual?

IN-CLASS WRITING

Adopting a Point of View   When you are writing a narrative, you have to know the point of view of your main characters. Look at the list of categories again and pick one that you are most interested in and most familiar with. Now imagine that you are planning a narrative about yourself in that role. Write an essay in which you explain (1) what your point of view in that role would be; (2) how people who think in a stereotyped way might view you.

For example, if you are a basketball player, you might write

(1) about your experiences and feelings as you get ready for a game and how you feel when your team is winning or losing, and (2) about what a spectator who thinks in stereotypes might imagine you to be feeling and thinking.

Building Sentences As you become more aware of your own point of view in a particular situation, you will also realize that you rarely act from just one attitude or role. You may protest a cut in funds for the basketball team not just because you are a player, but also because you are a member of the school community for which the games are an important social function. In addition, you might be speaking as a citizen concerned for the physical condition of your nation. As your thinking becomes more complex, you will find that you need more complex sentences to express your ideas.

The need for more complex thinking and writing is even more apparent when you try to get beyond stereotypes in thinking about other people. *It is the specific facts that are important.*

Stereotyped thinking is often expressed in simple sentences like *Teenagers are irresponsible.* When you want to discuss specific individuals, you realize that you cannot make such simple statements and that you need to add other ideas that modify the original thought. The sentence about teenagers might be a bit more accurate if it read *Teenagers are irresponsible* <u>*when they are first learning how to take charge of their own lives.*</u> The underlined words that have been added are called a *clause;* using clauses is one of the ways you can add ideas to a simple sentence. A clause looks like a sentence, for it has a subject (*they*) and a verb (*are . . . learning*), but it also includes a word that joins the ideas *when*). (You have had experience identifying subjects and verbs in Chapter 3. Look over these pages again if you want to refresh your memory.) These joining words are familiar to you; you have been joining ideas all your life without ever thinking about it. Now, however, you will want to become more aware of your use of them, know which ones best suit your writing needs, and learn how to cope with some of the problems they may raise.

The joining words you are most familiar with are *and* and *but.* These words are used to join two complete ideas so that they are equal in importance and strength. *And* is used to join additional information in a complete thought that is true along with the information in the first complete thought.

Example: Musicians explore new ways of expressing emotions through sound, *and* they increase our enjoyment of life as well.

But can be used when additional, unexpected information in a complete thought is joined to a previously stated idea that also forms a complete thought.

Example: John was the leading actor in the school drama club, *but* he was very shy about talking in class.

It is particularly useful to keep in mind the difference between these two words *and* and *but*. Look at the two sentences below:

She was bright and she was pretty.

She was bright but she was pretty.

What is the difference in meaning between these two sentences?

Exercise

From the list of categories on p. 101 choose three that interest you. Write two sentences for each. The first sentence should express an idea in a complete thought and then add a second idea, also a complete thought, that is equally true. Connect the two thoughts with *and*. The second sentence should express a complete thought that is true and then add a second complete thought that is an exception to the first. Connect the two ideas with *but*.

Often you may wish to add ideas to your sentences that are neither additions nor exceptions, but give information that would apply under certain conditions. There is a large group of joining words which you can use for this purpose. Some of these words, like *because*, *since*, and *so that*, are used when you want to add a reason or tell why the other idea in the sentence occurred.

Example: A wife will often scream at her husband *because* she has had a frustrating day with the children.

Other joining words, like *before*, *after*, *while*, and *when*, can be used when you want to indicate how time influences the event you are dealing with.

Example: Teenagers can act in a mature way *when* they are given responsibility.

When you want to join an idea that tells under what condition something occurred, joining words like *although*, *unless*, and *if* provide the means.

Example: *Unless* students feel they will not be put down by their teacher, they will not run the risk of making a mistake.

Below are some of the most common joining words:

after	how	till
although	if	unless
as	in order that	until
as if	provided (that)	when
as long as	since	whenever
as soon as	so that	where
as though	than	wherever
because	that	while
before	though	

Exercise

Below are several groups, each with two sentences. Join the two sentences together with the word in parentheses.

1. Joan washed all the dirty dishes. She finished her supper of fish and chips. (*as soon as*)
2. Maria and Yvonne went ice-skating at the local rink. George and Victor played basketball in the schoolyard. (*while*)
3. The mountains were covered with a dusky glow. The sun had set. (*after*)
4. Bob could not repair the broken bicycle behind the garage. He could not find the proper tools. (*because*)
5. Loretta wanted to go to the movies. She could not get tickets for the rock concert. (*since*)

Exercise

Using the categories on p. 101, write five sentences about five different groups. In each sentence, express an idea and then, using one of the joining words above, add another idea that gives some additional information.

When you have finished, underline the joining words in each sentence. Do you know how each of them affects the meaning of your sentence? What would happen if you changed the joining word? What is the difference in meaning between *Jane laughed although her boyfriend fell in the mud puddle* and *Jane laughed because her boyfriend fell in the mud puddle?* See how many sentences you can change the meaning of just by changing the joining word. (Sometimes you may have to make some minor changes in the form of the other words to make the sentence sound correct.)

Using joining words can cause problems in writing that you should be aware of. These words introduce units that look like complete sentences but in fact are not. In speaking we use them without difficulty, for we rely on other cues from our listeners to fill out the meaning. For instance, if you were to ask a friend why she couldn't go to the movies with you, she might answer, "Because I have to babysit for my sister." This answer looks like a complete sentence: it has a subject (*I*) and a verb (*have*) or (*have to babysit*). Yet, if you heard this sentence without knowing anything about the previous conversation, you might be confused. Standing by itself, the words *Because I have to babysit for my sister* suggest that some vital information has been left out — what is it that will (or will not) happen. The word *because* gives your reader the impression that some additional information is necessary to complete the thought of the sentence.

Exercise

Below are groups of "sentences." In each group, two of the three units can be joined. Depending on which of the two units you join, the emphasis of the sentence will be different. Rewrite each of the five groups so that there will be just two complete sentences in each one. Then rewrite each of the groups a second time, making a new combination. What is the difference in emphasis?

1. The boys will finish the job. When they get back from class. They will have enough time.
2. John failed chemistry. Although he studied all last night. He didn't understand the directions.
3. The movie was terrific. Although the actors weren't very good. We enjoyed the story.

4. Joe's girl friend walked out on him. After he danced with her best friend all evening. She told him she wasn't interested in him anymore.
5. Billy and Maria are going to the Pizza Hut. Unless you speak to them first. They will not know you are waiting for them at McDonald's.

Finish the following sentences by adding a second complete sentence unit. Notice that the joining word can come at the beginning or in the middle of the sentence.

1. When I am lonely
2. I feel sad when
3. After I have finished my homework
4. I drove the red Pinto after
5. My father cheered enthusiastically because
6. Because our school chorus gave a concert

READING

AFTER YOU, MY DEAR ALPHONSE —
Shirley Jackson

Mrs. Wilson was just taking the gingerbread out of the oven when she heard Johnny outside talking to someone.

"Johnny," she called, "you're late. Come in and get your lunch."

"Just a minute, Mother," Johnny said. "After you, my dear Alphonse."

"After *you*, my dear Alphonse," another voice said.

"No, after *you*, my dear Alphonse," Johnny said.

Mrs. Wilson opened the door. "Johnny," she said, "you come in this minute and get your lunch. You can play after you've eaten."

Johnny came in after her, slowly. "Mother," he said, "I brought Boyd home for lunch with me."

"Boyd?" Mrs. Wilson thought for a moment. "I don't believe I've met Boyd. Bring him in, dear, since you've invited him. Lunch is ready."

"Boyd!" Johnny yelled. "Hey, Boyd, come on in!"

"I'm coming. Just got to unload the stuff."

"Well, hurry, or my mother'll be sore."

"Johnny, that's not very polite to either your friend or your mother," Mrs. Wilson said. "Come sit down, Boyd."

As she turned to show Boyd where to sit, she saw he was

a Negro boy, smaller than Johnny but about the same age. His arms were loaded with split kindling wood. "Where'll I put this stuff, Johnny?" he asked.

Mrs. Wilson turned to Johnny, "Johnny," she said, "What is that wood?"

"Dead Japanese," Johnny said mildly. "We stand them in the ground and run over them with tanks."

"How do you do, Mrs. Wilson?" Boyd said.

"How do you do, Boyd? You shouldn't let Johnny make you carry all that wood. Sit down now and eat lunch, both of you."

"Why shouldn't he carry the wood, Mother? It's his wood. We got it at his place."

"Johnny," Mrs. Wilson said, "go on and eat your lunch."

"Sure," Johnny said. He held out the dish of scrambled eggs to Boyd. "After you, my dear Alphonse."

"After you, my dear Alphonse," Boyd said.

"After you, my dear Alphonse," Johnny said. They began to giggle.

"Are you hungry, Boyd?" Mrs. Wilson asked.

"Yes, Mrs. Wilson."

"Well, don't you let Johnny stop you. He always fusses about eating, so you just see that you get a good lunch. There's plenty of food here for you to have all you want."

"Thank you, Mrs. Wilson."

"Come on, Alphonse," Johnny said. He pushed half the scrambled eggs on to Boyd's plate. Boyd watched while Mrs. Wilson put a dish of stewed tomatoes beside his plate.

"Boyd don't eat tomatoes, do you, Boyd?" Johnny said.

"Doesn't eat tomatoes, Johnny. And just because you don't like them, don't say that about Boyd. Boyd will eat anything."

"Bet he won't," Johnny said, attacking his scrambled eggs.

"Boyd wants to grow up and be a big strong man so he can work hard," Mrs. Wilson said. "I'll bet Boyd's father eats stewed tomatoes."

"My father eats anything he wants to," Boyd said.

"So does mine," Johnny said. "Sometimes he doesn't eat hardly anything. He's a little guy, though. Wouldn't hurt a flea."

"Mine's a little guy, too," Boyd said.

"I'll bet he's strong, though," Mrs. Wilson said. She hesitated. "Does he . . . work?"

"Sure," Johnny said. "Boyd's father works in a factory."

"There, you see?" Mrs. Wilson said. "And he certainly has to be strong to do that — all that lifting and carrying at a factory."

"Boyd's father doesn't have to," Johnny said. "He's a foreman."

Mrs. Wilson felt defeated. "What does your mother do, Boyd?"

"My mother?" Boyd was surprised. "She takes care of us kids."

"Oh. She doesn't work, then?"

"Why should she?" Johnny said through a mouthful of eggs. "You don't work."

"You really don't want any stewed tomatoes, Boyd?"

"No, thank you, Mrs. Wilson," Boyd said.

"No, thank you, Mrs. Wilson, no, thank you, Mrs. Wilson, no thank you, Mrs. Wilson," Johnny said. "Boyd's sister's going to work, though. She's going to be a teacher."

"That's a very fine attitude for her to have, Boyd." Mrs. Wilson restrained an impulse to pat Boyd on the head. "I imagine you're all very proud of her?"

"I guess so," Boyd said.

"What about all your other brothers and sisters? I guess all of you want to make just as much of yourselves as you can."

"There's only me and Jean," Boyd said. "I don't know yet what I want to be when I grow up."

"We're going to be tank drivers, Boyd and me," Johnny said. "Zoom." Mrs. Wilson caught Boyd's glass of milk as Johnny's napkin ring, suddenly transformed into a tank plowed heavily across the table.

"Look, Johnny," Boyd said. "Here's a foxhole. I'm shooting at you."

Mrs. Wilson, with the speed born of long experience, took the gingerbread off the shelf and placed it carefully between the tank and the foxhole.

"Now eat as much as you want to, Boyd," she said. "I want to see you get filled up."

"Boyd eats a lot, but not as much as I do," Johnny said. "I'm bigger than he is."

"You're not much bigger," Boyd said. "I can beat you running."

Mrs. Wilson took a deep breath. "Boyd," she said. Both boys turned to her. "Boyd, Johnny has some suits that are a little too small for him, and a winter coat. It's not new, of course, but there's lots of wear in it still. And I have a few dresses that your mother or sister could probably use. Your mother can make them over into lots of things for all of you, and I'd be very happy to give them to you. Suppose before you leave I make up a big bundle and then you and Johnny can take it over to your mother right away. . . ." Her voice trailed off as she saw Boyd's puzzled expression.

"But I have plenty of clothes, thank you," he said. "And I don't think my mother knows how to sew very well, and anyway I guess we buy about everything we need. Thank you very much though."

"We don't have time to carry that old stuff around, Mother," Johnny said. "We got to play tanks with the kids today."

Mrs. Wilson lifted the plate of gingerbread off the table as Boyd was about to take another piece. "There are many little boys like you, Boyd, who would be grateful for the clothes someone was kind enough to give them."

"Boyd will take them if you want him to, Mother," Johnny said.

"I didn't mean to make you mad, Mrs. Wilson," Boyd said.

"Don't think I'm angry, Boyd. I'm just disappointed in you, that's all. Now let's not say anything more about it."

She began clearing the plates off the table, and Johnny took Boyd's hand and pulled him to the door. "'Bye, Mother," Johnny said. Boyd stood for a minute, staring at Mrs. Wilson's back.

"After you, my dear Alphonse," Johnny said, holding the door open.

"Is your mother still mad?" Mrs. Wilson heard Boyd ask in a low voice.

"I don't know," Johnny said. "She's screwy sometimes."

"So's mine," Boyd said. He hesitated. "After *you*, my dear Alphonse."

Discussion

1. What was Mrs. Wilson's attitude toward Boyd?
2. What was Johnny's attitude toward Boyd?
3. How does Mrs. Wilson's attitude reveal stereotyped thinking?

Writing an Argument Write a narrative about a situation in which two or more people have an argument because of their differing points of view. You can write about a disagreement between two friends, between parents and children, between a teacher and students, or any other situation that occurs to you. It can be a true story, or it can be made up.

Remember that in setting up your story you need to set the scene, and choose two or three events that you consider crucial. Then add to the telling of each of the events a few sentences that make the point of view of each character clear. If you are writing about an argument between a worker and a boss, you may want to show that the boss is only interested in getting a job done, while the worker is concerned with finishing early so as to get to a party on time. You can indicate the point of view of both by revealing their thoughts — how anxious the boss is to get the new merchandise on the racks so as to increase sales, for instance; on the other hand, you might show how the worker is eager to try out some new dance.

As you write, you will discover the complexity of character in each person you discuss. To express it, you will need complex sentences. Be sure to write several, using some of the joining words on p. 105.

Checklist for Use before Writing Final Draft

1. Is the point of view of each of the characters clear?
2. Is the conflict between the two characters apparent?
3. In supplying the relevant details of your narrative, have you answered the five W's?
4. Do the words you used heighten the emotions? Are they precise and vivid?
5. Have you varied your sentence structures by using joining words such as *but, because, when, while,* and so on?
6. Are your pronouns and verb endings correct?

Throughout your high school years you will be asked to write explanations of one sort or another — the causes of the Reformation, the potential influence of computers in the home, the effect of adding hydrochloric acid to a copper-nitrate solution. You have, of course, been giving explanations most of your life whether you were telling your brother how to change a tire or telling your teacher why your essay was late. And even after you finish school you will still need to explain situations and ideas, for instance, telling a new employee how the marketing section of your company operates or telling your employer how a change in advertising might increase sales. Even the writing you have done so far is often a form of explanation. Descriptions are explanations of how a person or an object looks to you and narratives are explanations of how an event occurred. The formal name for this kind of writing is exposition, and in the following units you will learn techniques for writing clear, concise, and interesting expository essays.

Chapter 9 will show you various ways of breaking down your material into categories and ways of developing a paragraph for each of them. Chapter 10 will show you how to select particular details for different purposes and how to unify each paragraph. In Chapter 11, you will learn ways to introduce your ideas in an interesting manner and at the same time to construct the thesis sentence, which is the sentence that tells your reader what your point of view is. All these elements are pulled together with a conclusion when you write the basic essay in Chapter 12. The next two chapters give you practice in two of the most common types of essays, the process essay and the comparison-contrast essay.

Since part of what makes your writing interesting depends on varied sentence structure, you will have a chance to learn to use a number of new patterns and to avoid some of the sentence errors that confuse and discourage your audience.

Chapter Nine

Sorting and Organizing

One of the difficulties of writing is deciding how to proceed from one sentence to the next, how to achieve a smooth flow of information and ideas in your essay. These problems can be solved by spending some time before you write grouping the thoughts that belong together into separate units. In an essay, the unit for such a grouping is the paragraph. In this chapter, you will discover a number of different ways to arrange your material. These methods will permit you to devise a composition with several paragraphs each of which deals with one aspect of your topic.

You will also learn to create more sophisticated sentences by using *who, which,* and *that,* and how to avoid the errors that sometimes arise with these patterns.

Written work is comprised of words that have been formed into sentences. But when we read a short story or an essay, we do not read lists of sentences. The sentences appear in units and these units or groups of sentences are called paragraphs.

Knowing where to end one paragraph and where to begin the next is difficult. The paragraph is not something that just happens. We will examine the reasons why writers shift from one paragraph to another. You have been writing paragraphs all term as part of the descriptive and narrative pieces you have composed. Your writing experiences have shown you that the paragraph itself rarely appears alone. It is almost always part of the larger piece of writing, but you need to understand exactly how the paragraph works. You need to know what sentences go in what paragraph. Therefore, in this chapter and in the next one, the paragraph will be discussed as a separate entity. Your writing assignments, though, will ask you to use paragraphs as part of the whole essay; this way, you will also begin to learn about the organization of different paragraphs within the whole essay.

ACTIVITY **Sorting Objects** Empty your pockets, purses, briefcases and book bags; put the items together in a central place. Now try to make some sense out of this seemingly unrelated pile of things. To do this you will have to come up with a category such as color, and then divide the objects according to several subdivisions within that category; for instance, all red items in one place, blue in another. See if you can divide the items using at least three different categories. Try sorting the items by use, or by cost, or by any other means you can come up with.

intro activity

Discussion

1. Did the categorizing help you make any sense out of the pile of items?
2. What did you learn about this group of people from each of the ways in which you categorized the items?
3. Was any one of your approaches to categorizing more useful or more interesting? Which one? Why?

LANGUAGE
LEARNING **The Paragraph** Perhaps when you sorted the objects, you categorized them by color — all of the green objects went in one pile, all of the red in another; or perhaps you sorted them by use — all of the items related to learning in one pile, all of the body-care items in another — but you did not put a green item in the red pile or a dictionary in the body-care pile. This kind of sorting is similar to what the writer does with ideas.

When you are writing about something, you have to organize or sort your information so that it will make some kind of sense to your reader. You do this by putting related ideas and information together.

In written work these groupings of related ideas are called *paragraphs*. A paragraph is a group of sentences all of which deal with one aspect of the topic you are writing about. For example, in an essay on the physical-education program at your school, you might have one paragraph on co-ed sports, one on male sports, and another on female sports. You might also have a paragraph on the strengths of the gym program and another on its weaknesses.

Paragraphs begin with an *indentation*. That is, you indicate that a new paragraph has begun by moving the first word of that paragraph several spaces in from the margin. This indentation is a signal to your reader. It says that a new idea or a different aspect of the topic is about to be discussed.

Exercise

Below is a list of objects found in the pockets, pocket-books, briefcases, and book bags of one group of students. Divide the items into two categories on your paper as shown on p. 118, and sort them into their proper places within each category.

1 blue chemistry book
1 green bottle of Brut after-shave
1 tortoiseshell comb
1 blue address book
1 pocket-size grey-green dictionary
1 brown wallet
1 red, white, and black matchbook
1 bottle wineberry nail polish
2 yellow spiral notebooks
1 white bottle of hand lotion
1 yellow bottle of hand lotion
1 green math textbook
1 black date book
2 Binaca mouth sprays
3 packs cigarettes
2 silver hair picks
16 orange and yellow composition texts
4 lipsticks in silver cases
3 blue looseleaf ring binders
1 red date book
1 green and yellow math textbook
1 copy *Jet* magazine
3 clear-glass and gold perfume bottles
1 yellow cigarette lighter
2 black mascara sticks
4 black combs
1 silver key ring with silver and gold keys
1 one-dollar bill

1 red wallet
1 copy of *Looking for Mr. Goodbar*

Category One — divided by ⎯⎯⎯⎯⎯

A. ⎯⎯⎯   B. ⎯⎯⎯   C. ⎯⎯⎯   D. ⎯⎯⎯   etc.
1.
2.
3.
etc.

Category Two — divided by ⎯⎯⎯⎯⎯

A. ⎯⎯⎯   B. ⎯⎯⎯   C. ⎯⎯⎯   D. ⎯⎯⎯   etc.
1.
2.
3.
etc.

Select one of the categories you have used. Then look at the items in one of the subsections. Write a paragraph in which you discuss what the items listed tell you about that group of students.

**LANGUAGE
LEARNING**   **Sentence Sorting**   Now let's do with ideas what we have just done with objects. What follows is an article entitled "Divorce — Teenage Style." The introduction and the conclusion of this article have been fully provided. The middle is jumbled.

1. Read the introduction carefully.
2. What three groups of ideas does the article deal with?
3. Draw up your paper with columns, as shown on p. 119. Label each column according to the three ideas the article discusses.
4. Now go over the jumbled list of sentences and fit each sentence into the category it belongs to.
5. Once you have separated the sentences into the three categories, try to order the sentences within each category so that the paragraph makes sense.

DIVORCE — TEENAGE STYLE

Opening paragraph: "I'll match you" is often heard at bars and at coffee counters. Each of the pairs matching stands a fifty-fifty chance of winning — or paying. In most cases, it doesn't matter who wins. The winner has a small instant pleasure and the loser a small, temporary disappointment. Now suppose the laws of chance shift and the odds of always losing are 51 percent and winning 49 percent. No smart gambler would even match for drinks or coffee. But thousands of teenagers are not smart gamblers, for they risk their future in marriages which studies in Indiana, Illinois, Michigan, and California have proved will fail 51 percent of the time. Follow-up depth studies have uncovered a single obvious reason for these failures: immaturity. And the three outstanding areas of immaturity are represented by money problems, in-law problems, and problems of unwanted children, for immature youth cannot deal with these three marriage problems.

Idea I	Idea II	Idea III

Conclusion: Matching for a drink or coffee is fun, and the pain of losing is temporary. Matching lives in a lasting marriage is a tougher gamble, and the pain of losing can extend through many years. If those under twenty could manage their money problems, deal with their in-laws, and make their unwanted children disappear, their marriages might turn out happy. But until the time comes, the smart money rides on marriage after the age of twenty.

Middle Paragraphs — Sentences to Be Sorted

Entertainment, vacations, insurance, barber, clothes, cosmetics, and time payments quickly gobble up the rest of the meager salary.

The groom's mother tells the bride how to cook, how to dress, how to think, and how to coddle her gem of a son.

Add medical costs, with one child born and another on the way, to complete the financial disaster.

But in destroying marriages, money problems sometimes can't compete with in-law problems.

The parents of the bride and groom can indeed heap pressures on a new marriage and destroy it.

Many teenagers succumb to social pressure; she marries to lend social acceptance to herself and an unwanted child.

The resentment brought on by such huge responsibility builds up, kills affection, and ends in divorce.

Even in cases where teenagers marry with their parents' blessing (rather than to escape parents), the immature couple still must work to establish their independence.

The car eats up $40 if paid for, $110 or more if not.

The bride's mother tells her how to "train" a husband, how many times a week to make love, how to prod the husband into another job, and how sorry it makes her that her daughter is wasting her life on an uneducated kid.

In most cases, top money for an untrained male teenager is $2.25 per hour, and this is a generous estimate.

Money is critical, and in-laws often want their way with grandchildren, but the major problem is the insecurity of the teenage girl who must marry the teenage father of her child.

A 40-hour week brings in $90; a second job, if there is one, $50 more — before taxes.

Both of the former problems are apt to interfere here.

But the restrictions of rearing children — the drudgery of scrubbing, washing, cooking, and satisfying the unending desires of children and husband — can overwhelm a mature woman, let alone a teenager who is suddenly driven into an unprepared-for adult pattern.

Even if a teenage couple can solve money and in-law problems, the pressure of unwanted children can spell the end of a marriage.

The first problem faced by the married teen couple is how to pay the bills.

An apartment costs $80 to $105 a month plus utilities.

Financial pressure is thus a prime cause of teenage divorce.

Food can easily account for $150.

Discussion

1. This is a carefully organized essay. The author has attempted to convince you not to marry before the age of twenty. Are you convinced?
2. Has the organization of the piece of writing helped to communicate the author's purpose? How?
3. Would you have done anything differently? What?

In the following article, James Tuite has described New York City in terms of its sounds. The article is presented here without any paragraphs. Divide the article into paragraphs.

 THE SOUNDS OF THE CITY — *James Tuite*

New York is a city of sounds: muted sounds and shrill sounds; shattering sounds and soothing sounds; urgent sounds and aimless sounds. The cliff dwellers of Manhattan — who would be racked by the silence of the lonely woods — do not hear these sounds because they are constant and eternally urban. The visitor to the city can hear them, though, just as some animals can hear a high-pitched whistle inaudible to humans. To the casual caller to Manhattan, lying restive and sleepless in a hotel twenty or thirty floors above the street, they tell a story as fascinating as life itself. And back of the sounds broods the silence. Night in midtown is the noise of tinseled honky-tonk and violence. Thin strains of music, usually the firm beat of rock 'n' roll or the frenzied outbursts of the discotheque, rise from ground level. This is the cacophony, the discordance of youth, and it comes on strongest when nights are hot and young blood restless. Somewhere in the canyons below there is shrill laughter or raucous shouting. A bottle shatters against concrete. The whine of a police siren slices through the night, moving ever closer, until an eerie Doppler effect brings it to a guttural halt. There are few sounds so exciting in Manhattan as those of fire apparatus dashing through the night. At the outset there is the tentative hint of the first-due company bullying his way through midtown traffic. Now a fire whistle from the opposite direction affirms that trouble is, indeed, afoot. In seconds, other sirens converging from other streets help the skytop listener focus on the scene of excitement. But he can only hear and not see, and imagination takes flight. Are the flames and smoke gushing from windows not far away? Are victims trapped there, crying out for help? Is it a conflagration, or only a trash-basket fire? Or, perhaps, it is merely a false alarm. The questions go unanswered and the urgency of the moment dissolves. Now the mind and the ear detect the snarling, arrogant bickering of automobile horns. People in a hurry. Taxicabs blaring, insisting on their checkered priority. Even the taxi horns dwindle down to a precocious few in the gray and pink moments of dawn. Suddenly there is another sound, a morning sound that taunts the memory for recognition. The growl of a predatory monster? No, just garbage trucks that have begun a day of scavenging. Trash cans rattle outside restaurants. Metallic jaws on sanitation trucks gulp and masticate the residue of daily living, then digest it with a satisfied groan of gears. The sounds of the new day are businesslike. The growl of buses, so scattered and distant at night, becomes a demanding part of the traffic bedlam. An occasional jet or helicopter injects an exclamation point from an unexpected quarter. When the wind is right, the vibrant bellow of an ocean liner can be heard. The sounds of the day are as jarring as the glare of a sun that outlines the canyons of midtown in drab relief. A pneumatic drill frays countless nerves with its rat-a-tat-tat, for dig they must to perpetuate the city's dizzy motion. After each screech of brakes there is a moment of suspension, of waiting for the thud or crash that never seems to follow. The whistles of traffic policemen and hotel doormen chirp from all sides, like birds calling for their mates across a frenzied aviary. And all of these sounds are adult sounds, for childish laughter has no place in these canyons. Night falls again, the cycle is complete, but there is no surcease from sound. For the beautiful dreamers, perhaps, the "sounds of the rude world heard in the day, lulled by the moonlight have all passed away," but this is not so in the city. Too many New Yorkers accept the sounds about them as bland parts of everyday existence. They seldom stop to listen to the sounds, to think about them, to be appalled or enchanted by them. In the big city, sounds are life.

Discussion

1. How did you divide the article?
2. Why did you begin each paragraph where you did?

Writing about Sounds of the Classroom At the signal from your instructor, be absolutely still for 5 minutes and listen to the sounds of your classroom. Write down all the sounds you hear.

Pick one way of categorizing these sounds and write a paper of at least three paragraphs on "The Sounds of a Quiet

Classroom." Begin each paragraph of your paper with a sentence that indicates which group of sounds you are writing about. Shift to a new paragraph each time you begin to write about a new category of sounds. Be as descriptive and detailed as you can.

Notice how many different ways you can group these sounds. Perhaps there were sounds in the room, sounds outside the room, and sounds outside the building. Maybe there were sounds made by people, by objects, by machines. There were also, most likely, loud sounds, soft sounds and mid-level sounds, shrill sounds and deep ones.

LANGUAGE LEARNING **Adding Clauses (Who, Which, That)** As you were writing about the sounds, you may have mentioned that you heard an airplane flying over the school and that the sound it made was a dull roar. You could have expressed this thought in two sentences by saying:

> I heard a dull roar. It came from an airplane flying over the school.

Or you may have combined these two sentences into one by writing:

> I heard a dull roar, which came from an airplane flying over the school.

The difference between the two methods is that in the second version the word *which* has been substituted for *it*. Thus, the word *which* acts both as a pronoun serving, as *it* did, to substitute for *airplane* and also as a linking word to join the two thoughts into one sentence. Other words which work in the same way are *who* (*whom, whose*), used when you are writing about people, and *that* used for either people or objects. *Which*, as you probably know, is used only for objects.

The advantage of using *who, which,* and *that* in your writing is that you can eliminate the many short sentences that give a choppy effect. The smooth flow of ideas from one category to another that you have achieved by good paragraphing will be further enhanced by the smooth flow of each sentence within the paragraph.

Exercise

Using *who, which,* or *that,* combine the two sentences in each of the following groups into one. Notice that you sometimes have a choice of ways to arrange your new sentence. As you can see from the example, you may need commas.

Example: Joan clutched her twirler's baton in her sweating palms. She smiled tensely at the faces in the crowd.

                Joan, who clutched her twirler's baton in her sweating palms, smiled tensely at the faces in the crowd.

                Joan, who smiled tensely at the faces in the crowd, clutched her twirler's baton in her sweating palms.

1. George will probably be made supervisor. He is very efficient.
2. Mopeds are becoming very popular. They can provide a good, cheap way of travelling.
3. Marian had never done much sewing. She tried to hem her new dress for Saturday night's party.
4. The old, abandoned house stood dark and forbidding in the winter moonlight. It looked as if it were haunted.
5. The man gave a great shout as the first runner appeared. He was father of the winner.

These words, *who, which,* and *that,* like the linking words you studied in Chapter 8, carry a promise to your reader that two complete ideas are being joined together. You must be careful then to see that there are, in fact, two complete thoughts; otherwise your reader will experience the sense of disappointment you feel over a broken promise. For instance, suppose you want to join the following two ideas: *The old fisherman stood motionless on the beach. He held the pole loosely but firmly in his right hand.* One way you could combine these ideas is: *The old fisherman, who stood motionless on the beach, held the pole loosely but firmly in his right hand.* But what if you ended your new sentence at the word *beach?* Then it would sound like this: *The old fisherman who stood motionless on the beach.* Your readers who have been prepared by the word *who* to expect two ideas, have only received one and want to know what more you had to say.

The simplest way to check your own writing is to skim through your paper, stopping every time you see a linking word. Then reread that sentence carefully, counting the complete thoughts to make sure there are two.

Exercise

Each of the following groups of words has one thought plus a linking word. Finish the sentence any way you wish making sure you have added a second complete thought.

1. Tony who was coming down the ski slope at a dangerously high speed
2. The two puppies that nipped each other playfully
3. The crowd that milled through the streets
4. The ten-speed bicycle that Joe wanted for Christmas
5. The little girl who raced noisily through the supermarket aisles

ACTIVITY Sorting Ideas

possible activity

can include discussion of purpose & audience

1. List on the board anything and everything you can think of about the high school you are now attending. Don't eliminate any of your thoughts. Include what your school offers, its facilities, its good points, its bad points, and anything else you can think of.

    You now have in front of you a body of information about a particular institution. What can you do to make some sense out of this collection of thoughts and ideas?

2. Let's observe what happens to our body of information when we organize according to a specific purpose.

    A. 1. Imagine that your school is underenrolled and in danger of closing down unless enrollment is increased. You have 2 more years until you graduate and you do not want this to happen, so you have joined a student-faculty committee that is going to write a brochure to convince grade nine students to select your school.

      2. Regroup the ideas you have on the board for this purpose.

      3. Eliminate any ideas which do not suit this purpose.

    B. 1. Now shift gears and imagine yourselves the students who have a number of complaints you wish to present to the administration. Your goal is to produce a pamphlet that will convince the entire student body to join you in a formal complaint to the current administration.

      2. Regroup the ideas on the board according to this purpose.

      3. Eliminate all ideas which do not fit with your goal.

What effect did purpose have on the groupings?
How did you know which group to place an idea in?
Was there one "right" way to group these ideas?

FORMAL
WRITING **Writing about Your School** In this essay you are going to be explaining things about your school. Select one of the two topics the class has just organized and grouped on the board — the brochure to convince students to attend your school, or the pamphlet to convince your fellow students to register a formal complaint.

Go over the groups of information that you have worked out on the board. Select the groups and the details within these groups that you want to include in your essay. Arrange these groups in the order in which you wish to present them. The order in which you arrange your information becomes the plan of your essay. It is your outline.

In order to decide what information to include and how to organize these groups of information, you will have to consider the purpose of your essay and the audience for whom you are writing this essay. If you are, for example, writing the pamphlet to convince high-school students to select your school you might want to highlight special features relating to your school's academic and sports reputation. You might also enrich the catalogue with some real situations real students have experienced. You may want to grab the potential students' interest right away. Otherwise, they may lose interest in what you have written and not bother to read any further. You'll have to think about what high-school seniors care about most. If you do decide to grab your reader immediately, you'll want to arrange your groups of information starting with the most important aspect and progressing to the least important. Or you might stagger your groupings with something of great interest followed by something of less importance — then back to something of greater importance. You shouldn't jump all over the place, though.

On the other hand, if you are writing a pamphlet to persuade your fellow students to join in a formal complaint, you might want to begin with a fairly serious problem first in order to get your readers' attention. But then you might go to the least serious issue and work up from there so as to end with the most important issue. In this way, you can get your readers fired up for action when they come to the end of your pamphlet. Your choice depends on the purpose of your essay and on who the readers of your essay will be. You may begin your paper with your strongest points and work to the weakest or least important, or you may build up to your most significant points.

Remember to keep your purpose always in mind as you write. Do not lie or exaggerate. Just use your information so that it suits your goal. Also consider who your audience is, and what they know and what they don't know.

You have a lot to consider when you write this essay. The information has been supplied. Your role is to work and mold this information into a useful and interesting piece of writing. Do not be surprised if it takes several tries to get this all together.

Checklist for Use before Writing Final Draft

1. Have you organized your essay so that each paragraph deals with one aspect of your subject?
2. Have you selected information that is appropriate to your purpose and your audience?
3. Have you used descriptive and narrative passages to strengthen the points you want to make? Are your words precise and persuasive?
4. Have you varied your sentence structure not only by using words like *and, but,* and *because,* but also *who, which,* and *that?*
5. Are your verbs and pronouns correct?

Chapter Ten

Finding the Main Idea

In the course of writing your paragraphs, you may have discovered that it was easier if you began with a sentence that told what the paragraph was going to discuss. This sentence, called the *topic sentence,* is an important ingredient in a paragraph, and much of the emphasis in this chapter centers on perfecting your skills in writing such sentences. You will also learn how to check a paragraph to be sure that the details actually support your topic sentence. Since smooth-flowing sentences are fundamental to your writing, you will learn additional methods for building sentence structure.

ACTIVITY

Follow up this activity by having students create own collage

Discovering Information in a Collage On pp. 130–131, you will find two collages. A collage is a visual composition made up of materials and objects that have been pasted on a surface. In the two collages presented here, the materials and objects were specifically selected and deliberately organized to communicate something about the individuals who created them. They were done in response to the question, "Who are you?" Look at the collages for a few minutes and see if you can tell what kind of people the student-artists thought they were.

Discussion

Select one of the collages to discuss first.

1. What is the most prominent item in the collage? Why do you think that item was chosen? What makes that item prominent? Is it its size? location?

2. What is the least prominent item in the collage? What makes it seem unimportant?
3. Are there several items in the collage that seem to relate to the same aspect of the artist's personality?
4. What overall impression of the artist do you get from this collage? Would you say, for instance, that this person is fun-loving or serious? emotional or rational? concerned with the past, present, or future?
5. From the items on the collage, what do you think are the artist's chief interests?

LANGUAGE LEARNING

Writing a Topic Sentence As you studied the collages on pp. 130–131, you discovered that there were certain main interests to which the student-artists devoted most of their attention. For each of these interests, there were several pictures and/or words that supplied particular details about those interests.

Using either the collage discussed in class or the other one, decide what were the three or four main interests of the artist and sort the information into categories as you did in the last chapter. In selecting the categories, try to find ones that are neither so broad that they cover almost all the information in the collage, nor so narrow that there is only one item of information to support them. For instance, in the collage on p. 131, the category *baby* would be too narrow for there is only one picture on that subject, but the category *family* would involve a number of different items.

Divide your page into categories, as shown below. Fit the information in the collage into the appropriate category.

Categories			
Details	1. 2. 3. 4. 5. 6. 7. 8.	1. 2. 3. 4. 5. 6. 7. 8.	1. 2. 3. 4. 5. 6. 7. 8.

But you are now faced with a new dilemma. How do you best present the information in the paragraph itself?

Each category you have set up is the *main idea* of the paragraph. The category is the *unifying theme* of this section or paragraph of your written piece. In writing we call this single main idea the *topic sentence*. This sentence, usually the first sentence of the paragraph, tells what aspect of the whole subject will be discussed and developed in this paragraph.

A good topic sentence introduces the reader to what the paragraph is about.

A good topic sentence limits the paragraph to one aspect of the whole subject.

Exercise

Write three topic sentences, one for each of the categories you set up in response to the collage.

If your topic sentences are workable, they will need to be backed up by more information. If a topic sentence says all there is to say about some aspect of your subject, it is too narrow. If a topic sentence talks about more than one idea, it is too broad. Check your topic sentences to see if they are workable.

A topic sentence is not a paragraph. It is not enough. It is a general statement which must be backed up. The specific details which you have listed under each category are the supporting details which will complete your paragraph.

Achieving Paragraph Coherence But once again you have choices to make. Yes, you have your topic sentence, but now you have to organize the specific details within the paragraph so that your paragraph makes sense and also makes for interesting reading.

In ordering details within a paragraph, you must consider the type of paragraph you are writing. In a descriptive paragraph you are presenting things in space and you can organize your information from near to far, far to near, right to left, left to right, top to bottom, bottom to top, most obvious to least obvious, prettiest to ugliest, etc. In a narrative paragraph your details have to do with events in time, so the most common organization here is chronological, that is, telling the events in the order in which they occurred. In the expository paragraph you are usually dealing with details that are reasons, so here you can move from what you consider most important to what you consider least important or the other way around. If you have a topic sentence reading *There are three major reasons why the decision was correct,* you will have to determine which reason to present first, second, and third.

Exercise

Go back to the details concerning the collage as you have categorized them.

1. Order the details in category 1.
2. Write up category 1 in paragraph form.
3. Compare your paragraph with the paragraphs written by your classmates. Discuss the reasons why you arranged the items within your paragraph the way you did.

ACTIVITY

Creating a Collage On a large sheet of cardboard create your own "Who Am I?" collage. Use pictures from magazines, photographs, wrappers, words, foods, material, objects — anything you can think of. Arrange the ideas you select so that they present a visual expression of who you are. *Do not put your name on the collage.*

Bring your collage to class. Once the collages are placed around the room, look them all over and select one that interests you. Do not choose your own.

IN-CLASS WRITING

Describing a Collage You have in front of you a collage done by one of your classmates, but you do not know by whom. The object now is to use the information in the collage to determine who made it. You will do this by figuring out what the collage communicates about the person who made it. Write up the collage just as the class wrote up the collage printed in this book. Include, though, a fourth paragraph in which you present your guess about who made this collage. A sample table is provided below to help you organize your writing:

	Categories		
Details			

Read your papers to one another.

Read the following selections; note how each author organized and developed the ideas within each paragraph.

ROOTS — Alex Haley

Just as it had been done in Africa, Kunta had also begun to keep track of the passing of time by dropping a small pebble into a gourd on the morning after each new moon. First he had dropped into the gourd 12 rounded, multicolored stones for the 12 moons he guessed he'd spent on the first toubob farm; then he had dropped in six more for the time he'd been here on this new farm; and then he had carefully counted out 204 stones for the 17 rains he'd reached when he was taken from Juffure, and dropped them into the gourd. Adding them all up, he figured that he was now into his nineteenth rain.

So as old as he felt, he was still a young man. Would he spend the rest of his life here, as the gardener had, watching hope and pride slip away along with the years, until there was nothing left to live for and time had finally run out? The thought filled him with dread — and determination not to end up the way the old man had, doddering around in his plot, uncertain which foot to put before the other. The poor man was worn out long before the midday meal, and through the afternoons he was only able to pretend that he was working at all, and Kunta had to shoulder almost all his load.

MEMORIES OF A CATHOLIC GIRLHOOD — Mary McCarthy

The temptation to try out some of my grandmother's beauty aids got the better of me when I was twelve. Unfortunately (like her household hints for a successful marriage), most of them had no bearing on my particular problems. "Not for the Youthful Skin" cautioned one astringent, and there was nothing in her crowded drawers for freckles. I did not need eyebrow pencil; my eyebrows were too thick already, and I had recently performed the experiment of shaving half of them off in the convent, while my grandparents were in California. My nose was my chief worry; it was too snub, and I had been sleeping with a clothespin on it to give it a more aristocratic shape. Also, I was bowlegged, and I was wondering about having an operation I had heard about that involved having your legs broken and reset. The dressing table offered no help on these scores, and, failing to find a lipstick and being timorous of the curling iron, I had to be satisfied with smearing a little paste rouge on my lips, putting dry rouge on my cheekbones (to draw attention away from the nose) and pink powder all over my face. I myself could see little change, but my grandmother could, and as soon as she came home that afternoon, a terrible scene took place, for I felt so guilty at what I had done that I would not admit that I had been "into" her dressing table, even when confronted with the proof in the disarranged drawers and the rouge that came off on the handkerchief she applied firmly to my cheek.

Discussion

1. What is the topic sentence of each paragraph?
2. How are the supporting details in each paragraph arranged?
3. Is there any information that does not belong in any of these paragraphs? Why?
4. Is there any place in any one of these paragraphs where the author should have started another paragraph? Where? Why?

Recognizing and Avoiding Run-on Sentences The basic rule of a sentence which you learned back in Chapter 3 stressed the notion that every sentence has a core made up of a subject and verb. In order to be correct, a sentence must have one, and no more than one, such core unless some sort of linking word is used to join a second subject-verb unit to the first. Much of the work on sentences that you have done so far has been designed to help you build on the basic core to write smoother sentences, conveying information in a more complex and sophisticated form. However, there is a risk that in your eagerness to write longer sentences you have forgotten to limit yourself to just one main subject-verb unit for each sentence. In writing about the collage, for instance, you might have had a sentence like this: *The artist is obviously interested in her family, she included many words and pictures about mothers and babies.* If you look closely at the sentence, you will see that there are not one, but two, subject-verb units — *artist is,* and *she included.* Since a correct sentence can only have one such unit unless there is a linking word, this is clearly not a correct sentence. In fact, it is two completely separate sentences, the first one ending at *family* and the second one starting at *she.* A comma was inserted to indicate a kind of break; often students sense that a break is occurring, but don't realize that a sentence has been completed. But using the comma does not remedy the situation; it is wrong to divide two sentences with a comma. Commas are extremely valuable marks of punctuation, but their use is limited to a few, fairly clearly defined situations (they are spelled out in the Appendix, in the section beginning on p. 228.) If you think you need a comma in a sentence, check to see if your situation matches one described in that section before you put it in.

In the example above, the mistake can be corrected by using a period after *family* and signalling the start of a new sentence by capitalizing *She.* The result, however, may not really seem satisfactory to you. The two sentences seem choppy, and the connection between them has been destroyed. A far better way to improve the sentence is to find a linking word that makes a logical connection. In this case *because, since,* or *for* would all be acceptable. When your teacher points out one of these sentence problems in your paper — they are called comma splice, fused sentences, or run-ons — you should try to recall what kind of connection you originally felt between the two parts of the unit and use a linking word that spells out that connection.

The correction of a run-on sentence can be challenging, and it is often difficult to catch run-ons before you hand in your paper. Count the subject-verb cores in each sentence and make sure you have a linking word if you have more than one core. Skim through your paper and underline every *he, she, they, I,* or *we* that appears near the middle of a sentence. Check to see if that sentence has a linking word. If there is none, you may have a run-on sentence. This method will not catch all run-ons, but it will pick up a surprising number.

Exercise

Correct the following sentences.

1. Joe had a good time he went to the movies.
2. Mary has a B+ average she works hard on her assignments.
3. There's a big sale at the record shop I bought five tapes for $10.
4. The twins went to each other's classes on April Fools' Day they completely fooled all their teachers.
5. We painted the car a beautiful deep purple we hoped our father would like it but he didn't.

Another reason students often write run-on sentences is that they mistake a number of words for linking words. Some of these words that look like linking words, but are not, are:

therefore	however
then	accordingly
here	there
nevertheless	in addition
consequently	now
moreover	finally
suddenly	thus
later	meanwhile

The above words are not words that can link sentence units together grammatically, though they are important in linking ideas. If you have been confusing them with linking words such as *because, although,* etc., you should study the list carefully until you are sure you can recognize them.

Exercise

The punctuation has been omitted from the following paragraph. Read it through and add the words and/or punctuation marks that will make it correct.

It had been 7 years since I had graduated from high school college seemed very strange As I stood in line at the bookstore to buy my texts I was shocked at how young my classmates appeared they seemed so carefree they didn't have a worry in the world I thought of my wife and children my job in the post office I couldn't neglect them even though I had added this new responsibility then in the freshman-composition class I felt even more different here the boys talked about the basketball team the girls giggled and flirted with the boys the first assignment was the toughest I was asked to describe myself to the class I tried to describe the years of dull frustrating jobs I tried to explain how much I hoped that college would improve my chances finally I tried to tell them how old I felt when I read my paper to the class I felt they still didn't understand what I was trying to say later a man came over to me I hadn't noticed him in the class before he said he had been out of school for 5 years and knew just what I meant suddenly I felt more relaxed I had found a friend.

READINGS

The major writing for this chapter will be to write on the topic "Who Am I?" The following readings will show you how some people who have thought and felt deeply about this question have responded. These selections are not models for you to imitate, but they may give you a sense of the many different ways people feel about themselves.

ON THE WAY TO BEING REAL — Barry Stevens

In the beginning, I was one person, knowing nothing but my own experience.

Then I was told things, and I became two people: the little girl who said how terrible it was that the boys had a fire going in the lot next door where they were roasting apples (which was what the women said) — and the little girl who, when the boys were called by their mothers to go to the store, ran out and tended the fire and the apples because she loved doing it.

So then there were two of I.

One I always doing something the other I disapproved of. Or other I said what I disapproved of. All this argument in me so much.

In the beginning was I, and I was good.

Then came in other I. Outside authority. This was confusing. And then other I became *very* confused because there were so many different outside authorities.

Sit nicely. Leave the room to blow your nose. Don't do that, that's silly. Why, the poor child doesn't even know how to pick a bone! Flush the toilet at night because if you don't it makes it harder to clean. Don't flush the toilet at night — you wake people up! Always be nice to people. Even if you don't like them, you mustn't hurt their feelings. Be frank and honest. If you don't tell people what you think of them, that's cowardly. Butter knives. It is important to use butter knives. Butter knives? What foolishness! Speak nicely. Sissy! Kipling is wonderful! Ugh! Kipling (turning away).

The most important thing is to have a career. The most important thing is to get married. The hell with everyone. Be nice to everyone. The most important thing is sex. The most important thing is to have money in the bank. The most important thing is to have everyone like you. The most important thing is to dress well. The most important thing is to be sophisticated and say what you don't mean and don't let anyone know what you feel. The most important thing is to be ahead of everyone else. The most important thing is a black seal coat and china and silver. The most important thing is to be clean. The most important thing is to always pay your debts. The most important thing is not to be taken in by anyone else. The most important thing is to love your parents. The most important thing is to work. The most important thing is to be independent. The most important thing is to speak correct English. The most important thing is to be dutiful to your husband. The most important thing is to see that your children behave well. The most important thing is to go to the right plays and read the right books. The most important thing is to do what others say. And others say all these things.

All the time, I is saying, live with life. That is what is important.

But when I lives with life, other I says no, that's bad. All the different other I's say this. It's dangerous. It isn't practical. You'll come to a bad end. Of course . . . everyone felt that way once, the way you do, but *you'll learn!*

Out of all the other I's some are chosen as a pattern that is me. But there are all the other possibilities of patterns within what all the others say which come into me and become other I which is not myself, and sometimes these take over. Then who am I?

I does not bother about who am I. I is, and is happy being. But when I is happy being, other I says get to work, do something, do something worthwhile. I is happy doing dishes. "You're weird!" I is happy being with people saying nothing. Other I says talk. Talk, talk, talk. I gets lost.

I knows that things are to be played with, not possessed. I likes putting things together, lightly. Taking things apart, lightly. "You'll never have anything!" Making things of things in a way that the things themselves take part in, putting themselves together with surprise and delight to I. "There's no money in that!"

I is human. If someone needs, I gives. "You can't do that! You'll never have anything for yourself! We'll have to support you!"

I loves. I loves in a way that other I does not know. I loves. "That's too warm for friends!" "That's too cool for lovers!" "Don't feel so bad, he's just a friend. It's not as though you loved him." "How can you let him go? I thought you loved him?" So cool the warm for friends and hot up the love for lovers, and I gets lost.

So both I's have a house and a husband and children and all that, and friends and respectability and all that, and security and all that, but both I's are confused because other I says, "You see? You're lucky," while I goes on crying. "What are you crying about? Why are you so ungrateful?" I doesn't know gratitude or ingratitude, and cannot argue. I goes on crying. Other I pushes it out, says "I am happy! I am very lucky to have such a fine family and a nice house and good neighbors and lots of friends who want me to do this, do that." I is not reasonable, either. I goes on crying.

Other I gets tired, and goes on smiling, because that is the thing to do. Smile, and you will be rewarded. Like the seal who gets tossed a piece of fish. Be nice to everyone and you will be rewarded. People will be nice to you, and you can be happy with that. You know they like you. Like a dog who gets patted on the head for good behavior. Tell funny stories. Be gay. Smile, smile, smile. . . . I is crying. . . . "Don't be sorry for yourself! Go out and do things for people!" "Go out and be with people!" I is still crying, but now that is not heard and felt so much.

Suddenly: "What am I doing?" "Am I to go through life playing the clown?" "What am I doing, going to parties that I do not enjoy?" "What am I doing, being with people who bore me?" "Why am I so hollow and the hollowness filled with emptiness?" A shell. How has this shell grown around me? Why am I proud of my children and unhappy about their lives which are not good enough? Why am I disappointed? Why do I feel so much waste?

I comes through, a little. In moments. And gets pushed back by other I.

I refuses to play the clown any more. Which I is that? "She used to be fun, but now she thinks too much about herself." I lets friends drop away. Which I is that? "She's being too much by herself. That's bad. She's losing her mind." Which mind?

NIKKI-ROSA — Nikki Giovanni

childhood remembrances are always a drag
if you're Black
you always remember things like living in Woodlawn
with no inside toilet
and if you become famous or something
they never talk about how happy you were to have
your mother
all to yourself and
how good the water felt when you got your bath
from one of those
big tubs that folk in chicago barbecue in
and somehow when you talk about home
it never gets across how much you
understood their feelings
as the whole family attended meetings about Hollydale
and even though you remember
your biographers never understand
your father's pain as he sells his stock
and another dream goes
And though you're poor it isn't poverty that
concerns you
and though they fought a lot
it isn't your father's drinking that makes any difference
but only that everybody is together and you
and your sister have happy birthdays and very good
christmasses and I really hope no white person ever has
cause to write about me because they never understand
Black love is Black wealth and they'll probably talk
about my hard childhood and never understand that all
the while I was quite happy.

UNWANTED — *Edward Field*

The poster with my picture on it
Is hanging on the bulletin board in the Post Office.

I stand by it hoping to be recognized
Posing first full face and then profile

But everybody passes by and I have to admit
The photograph was taken some years ago.

I was unwanted then and I'm unwanted now
Ah guess ah'll go up echo mountain and crah.

I wish someone would find my fingerprints somewhere
Maybe on a corpse and say, You're it.

Description: Male, or reasonably so
White, but not lily-white and usually deep-red

Thirty-fivish, and looks it lately
Five-feet-nine and one-hundred-thirty pounds: no physique

Black hair going gray, hairline receding fast
What used to be curly, now fuzzy

Brown eyes starey under beetling brow
Mole on chin, probably will become a wen
It is perfectly obvious that he was not popular at school
No good at baseball, and wet his bed.

His aliases tell his history: Dumbell, Good-for-nothing,
Jewboy, Fieldinsky, Skinny, Fierce Face, Greaseball, Sissy.

Warning: This man is not dangerous, answers to any name
Responds to love, don't call him or he will come.

SECOND NATURE — *Diana Chang*

How do I feel
Fine wrist to small feet?
I cough Chinese.

To me, it occurs that Cézanne
Is not a Sung painter.

(My condition is no less gratuitous than this remark.)

The old China muses through me.
I am foreign to the new.
I sleep upon dead years.

Sometimes I dream in Chinese.
I dream my father's dreams.

I wake, grown up
And someone else.

I am the thin edge I sit on.
I begin to gray — white and black and in between.
My hair is America.

New England moonlights in me.

I attend what is Chinese
In everyone.

We are in the air.

I shuttle passportless within myself,
My eyes slant around both hemispheres,
Gaze through walls

And long still to be
Accustomed,
At home here,

Strange to say.

THE CHANCE — *Harold Bond*

First grade. I am the skinny
one with the foreign accent. I am
so scared I think I will wee
in my pants. Miss Breen is teaching us
colors. We are cutting out
strips of paper in the fashion of
Indian feathers. We must

order them in descending hues on
a black headband. I cannot
understand Miss Breen. It is not done
the way it should be: blue with
yellow and black with white. Unless I
do something soon Miss Breen will
say I am a dumb Armenian. So

without looking I shuffle
my feathers in my hand. I paste them
over my headband. I spill
my pastepot, and I know I will wee
now because here comes Miss Breen,
only Miss Breen says, Good, Harold, good,
blue after purple and green

after blue. It happened, it happened
like a rainbow, like a swatch

of oil on water, eight feathers thieved
in perfect succession one
on the other, Miss Breen did not say
I am a dumb Armenian,
and I do not even have to wee.

AZTEC ANGEL — Omar Salinas

I
I am an Aztec angel
    criminal
        of a scholarly
           society
    I do favors
        for whimsical
           magicians
    where I pawn
      my heart
        for truth
    and find
      my way
  through obscure
      streets
    of soft spoken
        hara-kiris

II
I am an Aztec angel
    forlorn passenger
      on a train
    of chicken farmers
      and happy children

III
I am the Aztec angel
    fraternal partner
      of an orthodox
      society
    where pachuco children
      hurl stones
    through poetry rooms
and end up in a cop car
    their bones itching
    and their hearts
    busted from malnutrition

IV
I am the Aztec angel
    who frequents bars
spends evenings
        with literary circles
and socializes
        with spiks
niggers and wops
        and collapses on his way
            to funerals

V
Drunk
    lonely
        bespectacled
the sky
            opens my veins
            like rain
        clouds go berserk
            around me
        my Mexican ancestors
                chew my fingernails
    I am an Aztec angel
        offspring
        of a tubercular woman
        who was beautiful

Explaining Who You Are In this essay you are asked to explain who you are. Obviously, this is a very broad subject, so broad that at first you may find you either can think of nothing to say or of so much that you can't think where to begin. If you find yourself drawing a blank, look at the collage you made, at the answers you gave to the questionnaire on your interests in Chapter 8. If you find that you have a large number of isolated bits of information, you will need to develop some sort of categories in which to arrange your material.

Remember we are all very different. Though we often participate in the same activities and go to the same schools, each of us is unique and handles experiences in a special, personal way. It is your uniqueness that this paper is to be about. The following topics may help stimulate and organize your thinking.

1. What it was like to grow up female/male
2. What it was like to grow up black/white/Oriental/Indian/etc.
3. What it was like to grow up Catholic/Protestant/Jewish/Moslem/etc.
4. What it was like to grow up in the community in which you lived
5. What it was like to grow up poor/middle class/rich
6. What it was like to be the child of your parents
7. What it was like to be the brother of your sister(s)/sister of your brother(s)/brother of your brother(s)/etc.
8. What it was like to feel ugly/pretty/awkward/strong/smart/dumb/average/bored/alone/happy/together/etc.
9. What it is like today to be a male/female
10. What it is like today to be black/white/Oriental/Indian/etc.
11. What it is like today to be Catholic/Jewish/Protestant/Moslem/etc.
12. What it is like to live where you now live
13. What it is like today to be poor/middle class/rich
14. What it is like now to be the child of your parents
15. What it is like now to be the brother of your sister(s)/etc.
16. What it is like now to feel pretty/ugly/awkward/graceful/smart/dumb/average/bored/alone/happy/together/etc.
17. What it is like to be a high school student
18. What it is like to be a girlfriend/boyfriend
19. What it is like to be an uncle/aunt
20. What gives you joy/pleasure/satisfaction now
21. What gave you joy/pleasure/satisfaction in earlier years
22. What makes you angry now
23. What made you angry in your past
24. What it is like when you row a boat/swim/fish/hunt/walk/shop/dance/drink/smoke/laugh/cry/run/play tennis/play football/play basketball/etc.
25. And so much more . . .

Since this subject is so broad, you will have to decide how to narrow it down. There may be two or three aspects of your life that you consider most important. Jot down all the ideas you have gotten so far into separate columns as you have been doing in the past two chapters. Each of these categories will become a separate paragraph in your essay, for which you will want to construct a topic sentence. You may discover, however, that one aspect of your life is so significant that you want to write your whole paper on that subject. In that case you will want to find ways of breaking it into sections, perhaps dividing it into time periods — early childhood, recent past, and present; or seeing it in terms of your relationship with different people — your friends, your family, and your work or school supervisors. In any case be sure to include specific details and examples to make your essay clear and vivid.

Checklist for Use before Writing Final Draft

1. In telling who you are, have you focused on a few aspects of yourself?
2. Does each of your paragraphs deal with a separate aspect? Does each paragraph have a topic sentence? Does all the information in each paragraph support the topic sentence?
3. Have you used narration and description to emphasize your main points?
4. Are your sentences varied? Are they complete? Have you avoided run-on sentences?
5. Have you checked your verbs, pronouns?

Chapter Eleven

Beginning the Essay

All writing has a beginning, a middle, and an end. In expository writing, these sections are called the *introduction*, the *body*, and the *conclusion*. In this chapter you will concentrate on the introduction to the essay.

Beginnings are important in any kind of writing you do, for they represent your first appearance before your audience. Like any first impression, they establish an attitude, spark an interest, stimulate thinking. If your introduction is good, your readers will want to find out what you have to say on the subject. But in an expository essay, the introduction has two further tasks to perform. One is to tell your readers the topic of the essay. For example, your topic might be education, or early-childhood education or nursery schools during the 1940s. The other is to tell what direction your essay will be moving in. For example, you might want to prove that the early-childhood center in your town is excellent or that during the 1940s nursery schools did very little to educate children. This statement of direction is called the *thesis*.

A clearly stated essay topic, a precise thesis, and a stimulating introduction will guarantee your readers' interest in your essay.

ACTIVITY **Thinking about Favorite Activities** On a sheet of paper, list twenty things that you really like to do. Do it quickly, writing down the first things that come to your mind. This is your private list, which no one else will see. On it you should put things that you enjoy, make you happy, are fun, and make you feel good. You do not have to put the items in order of importance, and if you cannot think of twenty things, just list as many as you can.

Part I

After you have completed your list, draw a chart like the one below and add the following information, using the indicated symbols.

A/P   Is this an activity done alone or with people? Write A if it is done alone, P if it is done with people.

$5   Does this activity cost more than $5? Put a $ in the column for all that do.

public   Would you discuss this activity in public? Put a check in the column for all those that you would.

2 years   Would the activity have been on your list two years ago? Put a check in the column for all that would have been.

F   Do you think your father would include the activity on his list? Put a check in the column for all that you think he might have mentioned.

M   Do you think your mother would include the activity on her list? Put a check in the column for all that you think she might have included.

Date   Write the approximate date you last did each activity.

O   How often in the past year have you done this activity? Put *vo* for *very often*; *o* for *often*; *s* for *seldom*; *n* for *never*.

Rank   Number from 1 to 5 the ones you like to do best. Use 1 as the top.

	A/P	$5	Public	2 years	F	M	Date	O	Rank
1.									
2.									
3.									
4.									

1. In what ways have you changed your interests in the past few years?

2. In what ways are you different from your parents?
3. Does your list show you to be a person who likes to be with other people, or does it show that you prefer to be alone? Do you think that your list reflects you accurately? Why?

Part II
Now make a list of everything you did last weekend from Saturday morning at 8:00 A.M. until Sunday midnight. You will not have to show the list to anyone. Compare this list with the first one you made. Put an x next to all the activities that were on both lists. Put a check next to all the activities that you like to do that you did not do last weekend. Circle all the activities you did last weekend that are not on your list of favorites.

1. What did you learn from comparing these two lists?
2. Which of the two lists do you think reflects the "real" you? Why? How can you explain the differences between the two lists?

IN-CLASS WRITING

Focusing on a Topic Write three paragraphs in response to one of the two following statements:

1. I never get a chance to lead the life I want to.
2. I manage to do most of the things I prefer to do.

You will need to think of *three* reasons to support the statement you select. You might, for instance, choose three activities you have been unable to engage in and then discuss the reason why each of them has been impossible. For instance, if one reason is that a given activity is too expensive, you might mention how the lack of part-time jobs has cut down your income. If you don't have time for the second activity, you could discuss the hours you have to spend on homework. A third activity might be impossible because your community lacks the necessary facilities.

LANGUAGE LEARNING

Finding a Topic The in-class writing assignment was chosen because it forced you to concentrate your attention on a particular topic. Since you were confined to discussing why you could or could not do certain things you wanted to do, you could not wander into outside matters. If you were writing about why you haven't had a chance to go skiing, you would not devote most of your writing to the joys of swooping down a mountain of fresh powder, however much you started thinking about it. You might say that both ideas deal with skiing, but the topic given in the assignment was much narrower than skiing. If you think about it for a moment, a topic like skiing is big enough for a whole book, even two or three books. Since your assignment was to write only a paragraph, you could only treat one small aspect of the entire subject.

For your own essays, you will want to pick topics that can be handled in the number of pages you are planning to write. You can cover only a small aspect of skiing in a 2-page essay; even a 10-page essay can only cover a part of the whole subject.

Exercise

The titles writers give to their articles usually give an indication of the general subject and the particular aspect they are planning to discuss. Look at the following titles and then name the general subject and guess what the specific topic might be.

title: *Raising Hell on the Highways*
    subject:
    specific topic:

title: *Is There Any Knowledge That a Man Must Have?*
    subject:
    specific topic:

title: *Fathering: It's a Major Role*
    subject:
    specific topic:

Compare your answer with your classmates'.

Discussion

1. How does specific topic differ from subject?
2. How is specific topic similar to subject?

Exercise

From the list of twenty things you like to do, pick three you might want to write an essay about and write a phrase or sentence that gives a specific topic. At first glance they may seem to be adequate as topics, but you probably realize now that you wouldn't be able to say everything you know in one short essay. For instance, if you plan to write about dancing, you could not cover everything in just a few paragraphs. Decide what particular aspect you want to cover. That will become the topic of your essay.

activity (topic or general subject)
    specific topic:

activity
    specific topic:

activity
    specific topic:

Writing a Thesis Finding a workable topic gives you a good start on your essay. As you were searching, you probably were already getting some ideas about what you wanted to say. If you had been thinking about discos and had decided to limit yourself to the kinds of music played in different clubs, you may have been thinking about which kinds are best for your style of dancing. In other words, you were not only finding your topic, you were also deciding what direction your essay might move in. You were deciding not just on kinds of music, but also what kind is best for you. You were, in effect, formulating your *thesis*.

The thesis is the most important part of your essay. It tells your readers what the purpose of your paper is, what point you are going to prove, what they may expect to gain from reading your essay. And it gives you a focus for organizing your thoughts. You might think of your thesis as if it were a judge's decision in a court case. The decision is the point of the judge's report; everything else to be said on the subject has to supply reasons supporting that decision. Your thesis should provide a similar focus for the rest of your essay.

Beginning writers often hesitate to make clear thesis statements because they fear they might be challenged. But the more pointed your thesis, the more interest you arouse in your readers. If you were writing about the sports activities at your school, you might think of a thesis sentence such as *There are many views of sports activities at Hillcrest High*. But a sentence like that really doesn't give your reader any sense of what your view is. If you say *sports activities at Hillcrest High are very active*, you and your reader both know what you have to prove in the body of your essay. There may be students who will argue with you, but your essay is not the last word on the subject; it is just your reasoned opinion on it.

Exercise

Below are a number of topics to be discussed in an essay, followed by supporting ideas. Compose a thesis sentence for each essay.

1. "The Value of a College Education" (topic)
   to earn more money in the future
   to develop interests that bring lifelong satisfaction
   to improve your ability to serve the community
   Thesis sentence: _____
2. "The Pleasure of Motorcycles"
   tests skills and reflexes
   gives sense of personal freedom
   teaches user basic mechanics
   Thesis sentence: _____
3. "The Advantages of Marriage"
   provides security
   ensures safe way to raise children
   provides companionship
   Thesis sentence: _____

In the exercise on p. 152 you wrote topics. Now write a thesis sentence for each of these topics.

LANGUAGE LEARNING

Writing the Introduction Now that you have learned to state a workable topic and create a thesis, you only need to learn how to put your introduction together so as to stimulate your readers' interest. The easiest way is to be as clear and concise as possible. Introductions don't have to be very long. For most student essays, in fact, four or five sentences are all that is needed. In those sentences you want to let your readers know what your specific topic is, what your thesis is and give them some reason why they should be interested in it.

One method many writers use successfully is to begin by mentioning a slightly broader topic than the one you will be discussing. If you are planning, for instance, to discuss your favorite rock singer, you might begin by mentioning a number of rock singers who are currently popular in your area. You don't have to get any broader than that. You certainly would not want to begin by discussing all music, or even all rock music. You might mention three or four singers, pointing out their special characteristics. The final sentence, your thesis, would then point out the particular qualities of the person you are going to write about. Your introductory paragraph might look like this:

> Although the country-rock-music craze has slowed down North America, a number of women vocalists continue to attract a wide following. Dolly Parton, the Tennessee Mountain Girl, sways audiences today as she has been doing for years with her solid, deceptively simple style. Anne Murray's warm, clear voice captures the "down home" feeling perfectly, and Linda Rondstadt's tough authenticity sparkles in the social realm. But the most appealing of them all is Emmylou Harris, whose haunting tones bring drama into every song she sings.

This form of introduction uses what sometimes has been called the "inverted-triangle approach" because it gradually narrows the range of interest from a broad idea to the specific point. In our example the triangle would look like this:

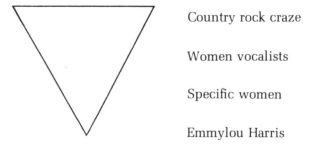

Country rock craze

Women vocalists

Specific women

Emmylou Harris

Exercise

For one of the three activities for which you have written topics and thesis sentences, write an introduction using the inverted-triangle approach.

This method of writing an introduction is only one of several ways of beginning. Read the following introductions and see how these writers begin their essays.

"Fathers are a biological necessity but a social accident," Margaret Mead once observed. Contemporary women might take issue with this traditional image of the father as the helpless parent with little talent for or interest in child-rearing. They are likely to argue that the father is just as capable of caring for babies as the mother, and ought to at least share the burdens.
(Ross D. Parke and Douglas B. Sawin, "Fathering—It's a Major Role.")

Everyone lives on the assumption that a great deal of knowledge is not worth bothering about; though we all know that what looks trivial in one man's hands may turn out to be earth-shaking in another's, we simply cannot know very much, compared with what might be known, and we must therefore choose. What is shocking is not the act of choice which we all commit openly but the claim that some choices are wrong. Especially shocking is the claim implied by my title: There is some knowledge that a man *must* have.
(Wayne Booth, "Is There Any Knowledge That a Man Must Have?")

Americans are strangely sentimental about the heavy, long-distance truck — the tractor-trailer outfit with a dozen or so gears and a dozen or so tires that washes the highways with waves of terrible noise and vibrations and towering arrogance. Trucks now carry about one-third of the nation's intercity merchandise, and we probably could not do without them, but they are nonetheless one of the great abominations of the Asphalt Age.
(Robert Sherrill, "Raising Hell on the Highways.")

Discussion

1. What was the topic for each essay?
2. What was the thesis?
3. What kinds of information did the writer give in the introduction?
4. How would you describe the author's approach?

FORMAL WRITING **Writing on a Favorite Activity**   Write an essay on some aspect of one of your favorite activities. You may want to use one of those for which you have already found a topic, created a thesis sentence, and constructed an introduction, but you are free to choose another if you wish. Be sure, however, that your topic is not too broad for a 2- or 3-page essay, and that your thesis sentence gives you something definite to prove.

If you decide to write on how to get started in skiing, you should have two or three main ideas, each of which can be discussed in a separate paragraph.

Checklist for Use Before Writing Final Draft

1. Does your essay have a thesis which limits your subject to a workable size and presents a viewpoint that needs to be supported?
2. Does this thesis come at the end of an introductory paragraph?
3. Does the topic sentence of each paragraph present an aspect of your thesis and do the details support the main idea of that paragraph?
4. Have you used description and narration to clarify the points you are making?
5. Are your sentences, verbs, and pronouns correct?

Chapter Twelve

Writing the Whole Essay

In this chapter, you will concentrate on how to write a conclusion as well as on how to put the whole essay together. You will have two short in-class writing assignments. In the first, you will be asked to write a conclusion; in the second, you will be asked to write an introduction and a conclusion. The *major writing* will be a 500-word essay in which you discuss who and where you will be ten years from now. In this writing assignment you will draw together all that you have learned about writing a composition.

ACTIVITY **Stopping an Argument** You have very probably been in the company of friends, acquaintances, or even strangers when an argument developed between two of them. Did you see how it spiralled from a casual disagreement to an angry confrontation over a matter that had seemed quite insignificant? Once positions hardened, tempers and voices rose, veins appeared and muscles contracted; after jockeying for space the two adversaries really squared off when, all of a sudden, out of nowhere, a voice of reason and calm prevailed. Someone stopped the argument.

Directions

In this activity, two participants will stage an argument that will require the intervention of the teacher.

The participants play friends attending different high

schools. Not once in the past year have they had a serious disagreement. Next Thursday, spring vacation begins. One of them has made secret plans for both to go south together on a school-sponsored excursion for a week of swimming, waterskiing, and beachcombing. The other has made equally secret plans for the two to go on a similarly sponsored excursion to the north woods for a week of hiking, skiing, and camping. Each made plans without consulting the other beforehand, thinking the other had no place to go and probably didn't have the deposit money. Besides, both based their decisions on their own sports preferences.

The two participants can begin the argument. They may build up as much steam as they wish. But they must stop when the teacher calls, "Stop!"

Discussion

1. Did the participants convince you that their argument was serious enough to involve your attention?
2. Describe the tone and mood of the participants at the point they were stopped.
3. Would you describe as "natural" your curiosity to know how the argument would finally be resolved?
4. In what way is the following situation comparable? Your father is reading page 1 of the Sunday paper. Your sister has just left the house with page 27 wrapped about a peach pie she is taking to a friend. The story your father is reading continues on page 27.
5. Describe how you felt having the teacher stop the argument.
6. Which person do you think would have won the argument? Explain what you call "winning" in such a context.

IN-CLASS WRITING **Finishing the Argument** Write a brief paragraph picking up only one of the threads of the argument at the point where it was stopped. Explain what reasoning would eventually convince one roommate to go along with the other's plans.

LANGUAGE LEARNING **Writing Conclusions** Perhaps not all writers, but certainly many — whether they are beginners like yourself or veterans — frequently find it nearly as difficult to end an essay as they did to begin it. We have all experienced that sudden jolt of surprise, disappointment, or indignation, when we suddenly see the list of characters appear on the screen or watch the curtain ring down, signalling *The End* while we were still absorbed in the action of the story. If we feel that our feelings and expectations have been manipulated, the writer has withheld something from us that might have prepared us for the ending. Most often, after we have had time to think back on the development of the story and its characters, we can agree that the writer was trying to achieve a specific purpose. When the writer's purpose seems clear, we may disagree with him, but we accept more readily what he or she tells us.

Unlike the playwright or scriptwriter, when you write an expository essay, you need not be concerned with achieving an effect. You will, however, be concerned with making your point clearly and logically, and with convincing your reader that you are serious and you know what you are talking about. Just as there are definite procedures to follow for writing an effective body and introduction, so there are procedures to follow for writing a conclusion. On the other hand, there are some very specific things to avoid. Let's then begin with the *don'ts*:

1. *Don't just stop.* How are readers to know you're really finished and there isn't more to come somewhere on a page they don't have?
2. *Don't conclude with a detail.* Details are important to the body of your essay, but you don't want to end your essay with one.
3. *Don't bring up a new point in your concluding paragraph.*
4. *Don't end with an apology.* This is the easiest way possible to convince your reader you don't know what you're talking about.

Now, you know what you shouldn't do. How, then, should you end your essay? What is the appropriate conclusion that will neatly tie all your main points together and deliver to your readers that satisfying sense of completion? Most writers find, as you probably will, too, that the *summary conclusion* is the most common ending for expository essays.

The summary conclusion is the kind that ends an expository piece by going back over the main ideas stated in the body and by restating the thesis statement. If you choose the summary conclusion, you should keep in mind the length of your essay. One or two sentences in which you restate your thesis may be entirely sufficient when your essay is 2 pages or under. Although your conclusion may be only a couple of sentences, do not forget to indent so that your reader is given a proper signal that you are moving into a new paragraph. Cue words such as *finally, in short, in sum, thus,* and *therefore* indicate to your reader that you are concluding your essay. Concluding paragraphs are necessarily short since they do not develop an idea as the paragraphs in the body of your essay do.

When your essay is longer, consisting, say, of a body of at least three fully developed paragraphs, a summary consisting of three sentences or more may be sufficient. You may use such lead-off words as *to sum up, lastly, on the whole, as I have said,* and *in conclusion* to open the first sentence of your longer summary paragraph. What is most important, though, in any summary conclusion, is to keep your reader's attention on the thesis statement.

You have other options for concluding your essay, too. Rather than summarize or look back, you can propel your reader forward to new considerations, new implications, possible solutions, even to a call for immediate action.

Read carefully some of the following examples of the kinds of conclusions you might find appropriate:

1. *The short, one- or two-sentence summary:*

> In short, if you're looking for inexpensive, but adventurous summer travel, I heartily recommend hitchhiking.

The writer's thesis statement was: *Hitchhiking is one way of spending a summer vacation without spending much money.*

2. *A summary conclusion for the longer essay:*

> To sum up, we can see that as our technology keeps expanding, the disadvantages may soon outweigh advantages. We have seen how various kinds of pollutions plague our cities as well as our rivers and lakes and countryside. We have seen the disruption of the natural balance between wildlife and its habitat, and how the imbalance eventually affects our weather and climate. Finally, we explored the disruption of the traditional family and how the consequences affect our way of life.

The writer's thesis statement was: *Pollution of our cities and countryside, the disruption of the natural balance between wildlife and its habitat, and the altering of traditional family life* prove that the disadvantages of our expanding technology may soon outweigh the advantages.

3. *Considering the implications:*

> In sum, the result of all this is clear. How can we say we have a free and equal society when half the population cannot enjoy the same privileges as the other half? Sure, I would love to hitchhike across the country during the summer. I want to save money. I have health, energy, and a sense of adventure. But the society I live in tells me in so many words that I would be insane to attempt such a trip, because I'm a woman. We need to look deeper into the meaning of freedom from fear as one of the freedoms our Constitution guarantees.

The writer's thesis statement was: *I would like to hitchhike across the country, maybe alone, but the freedom to do so is not granted to women.*

4. *Finding a solution:*

> Consequently, as we've seen, there is really only one solution to the problem of finding the perfect summer vacation. Don't take any. Get a job. Not only will you earn money instead of spending it, which in turn may well make you financially independent for most of the year, but you will probably meet just as many interesting people and have an occasional adventure, to boot. What could possibly make summer vacation more rewarding?

The writer's thesis statement was: *Finding the perfect summer vacation may pose a few problems, but keep looking, you'll find it.*

5. *Calling for action:*

> Thus, we have seen that everything the politicians and sociologists have prescribed has proven to be generally ineffective. As I see it, the only way to reduce crime in our cities is for all of us as citizens to take active steps to rid ourselves of those who beat, mug, rob, rape, and kill. I am not suggesting vigilante groups or arming ourselves to the teeth, but in order to defend ourselves and to protect those we love, I say

we organize to plan and act. We must use every available municipal agency to advise and assist us. The time is now; we must act at once.

The writer's thesis was: *Fighting urban crime successfully demands planning, organizing, and taking action.*

You may find other ways of rounding off your essays that are equally suitable. You may never in your life use *in conclusion* or *to summarize*, but why not use all the options at your command until you find those that work best for you?

Using the Active and Passive Voices Writing forcefully and effectively is possible only when you can make words and sentences achieve your purpose in any written assignment. Sometimes you want a subtle shade of meaning; sometimes you may want to suggest violent action. Knowing the difference between *active* and *passive* sentences and knowing when to use each in different contexts enable you to achieve each of these effects.

An *active sentence* is one in which the subject is the performer of the action, for example:

$$\underline{\text{S}} \quad \underline{\text{V}} \qquad \underline{\text{C/ROA}}$$

The sheriff drove the old prospector out of town.

The sheriff is the subject of the sentence; *drove* is the past tense form of the verb *drive;* and *the old prospector* is the noun *complement* and the *receiver* of the action.

A *passive sentence* is one in which the subject is the receiver of the action, for example:

$$\underline{\text{S/ROA}} \qquad \qquad \underline{\text{V}}$$

The old prospector was driven out of town by the sheriff.

Notice the difference between the two renderings: In the passive sentence, the complement or receiver of the action of the first sentence becomes the subject. Notice the verb form: The past tense of the verb *to be* is used together with the past participle of the verb *drive. The sheriff,* which was the subject of the previous sentence, now follows the verb, and is preceded by the word *by.* You may also write the passive form like this: *The old prospector was driven out of town.* As you see, *by the sheriff* has been omitted; the main point is not lost, because in a passive sentence the focus of meaning has shifted to what has happened rather than who did it.

Active sentences have a more immediate impact because they present direct action:

Mary Lou slapped Debbie.

Hal caught the high-fly ball.

A cold spell struck the nation yesterday.

But when we change active sentences to passive sentences, we lose the sense of direct, immediate action:

Debbie was slapped (by Mary Lou).

The high-fly ball was caught (by Hal).

The nation was struck by a cold spell yesterday.

Only the third sentence does not lose force and immediacy when it's shifted to the passive form. But notice too that it's the only sentence which requires the by phrase to complete the meaning. Now look at the following sentences and see how each gains by being written in the passive:

In the course of a few days, summer was gone.

We were informed by letter that we would not be rehired.

Pélé was photographed, alone on the field, his hands covering his face, crying.

Newspaper writers make frequent and effective use of passive sentences when the focus is on what happened or to whom something happened, especially when the person involved is either a well-known figure or is not identified:

One person was killed and two were injured yesterday when a milk van collided with a Volkswagen near Exit 11 on the Merrick Parkway.

Bobby Deerfield, Grand Prix winner, was taken into custody this morning on charges of assault and mayhem.

An unidentified man was apprehended and prevented from creating a disturbance at the entrance to the Gordie Howe arena today.

When referring to a person you can't identify or who isn't important to the point you're making, it is usually better to write passive sentences rather than active sentences with the frequently used subject they. Look at the following examples:

They told me I should take my form to the principal's office.

They should not make people wait in line for hours.

They told me I would have to make an appointment with the counsellor.

Each of these sentences could benefit by being in the passive:

I was told to take my form to the principal's office.

People should not be made to wait in those long lines.

I was told to wait for the counsellor.

In changing the five sentences below from active to passive, be sure you use the correct form of the verb *to be* plus the past participle of the main verb. Decide whether or not you need to use the *by* phrase to complete the meaning:

1. They told Alice to bring her W-2 form with her.
2. The police of Greene Township fined Barnaby Jackson yesterday for speeding on Highway 80.
3. A car struck and killed Jimmy's puppy, Duke.
4. The city tow company towed my car away while I was shopping this morning.
5. Somebody told me that Mr. Withers was not seeing any more applicants.

READING   Keeping in mind all you have learned about developing a main idea and satisfying a reader's need to know there is a beginning, middle, and end in a piece of writing, read the story "Wet Saturday," by John Collier, and see if all of these elements are present. If any is absent, do you experience a jolt or uneasiness as a result?

WET SATURDAY — John Collier

It was July. In the large, dull house they were imprisoned by the swish and the gurgle and all the hundred sounds of rain. They were in the drawing room, behind four tall and weeping windows, in a lake of damp and faded chintz.

This house, ill-kept and unprepossessing, was necessary to Mr. Princey, who detested his wife, his daughter, and his hulking son. His life was to walk through the village, touching his hat, not smiling. His cold pleasure was to recapture snapshot memories of the infinitely remote summers of his childhood — coming into the orangery and finding his lost wooden horse, the tunnel in the box hedge, and the little square of light at the end of it. But now all this was threatened — his austere pride of position in the village, his passionate attachment to the house — and all because Millicent, his cloddish daughter Millicent, had done this shocking and incredibly stupid thing. Mr. Princey turned from her in revulsion and spoke to his wife.

"They'd send her to a lunatic asylum," he said. "A criminal-lunatic asylum. We should have to move away. It would be impossible."

His daughter began to shake again. "I'll kill myself," she said.

"Be quiet," said Mr. Princey. "We have very little time. No time for nonsense. I intend to deal with this." He called to his son, who stood looking out of the window. "George, come here. Listen. How far did you get with your medicine before they threw you out as hopeless?"

"You know as well as I do," said George.

"Do you know enough — did they drive enough into your head for you to be able to guess what a competent doctor could tell about such a wound?"

"Well, it's a — it's a knock or blow."

"If a tile fell from the roof? Or a piece of the coping?"

"Well, guv'nor, you see, it's like this ——"

"Is it possible?"

"No."

"Why not?"

"Oh, because she hit him several times."

"I can't stand it," said Mrs. Princey.

"You have got to stand it, my dear," said her husband. "And keep that hysterical note out of your voice. It might be overheard. We are talking about the weather. If he fell down the well, George, striking his head several times?"

"I really don't know, guv'nor."

"He'd have had to hit the sides several times in thirty or forty feet, and at the correct angles. No, I'm afraid not. We must go over it all again. Millicent."

"No! No!"

"Millicent, we must go over it all again. Perhaps you have forgotten something. One tiny irrelevant detail may save or ruin us. Particularly you, Millicent. You don't *want* to be put in an asylum, do you? Or be hanged? They might hang you, Millicent. You must stop that shaking. You must keep your voice quiet. We are talking of the weather. Now."

"I can't. I . . . I. . . ."

"Be quiet, child. Be quiet." He put his long, cold face very near to his daughter's. He found himself horribly revolted by her. Her features were thick, her jaw heavy, her whole figure repellently powerful. "Answer me," he said. "You were in the stable?"

"Yes."

"One moment, though. Who knew you were in love with this wretched curate?"

"No one. I've never said a —— "

"Don't worry," said George. "The whole god-damned village knows. They've been sniggering about it in the Plough [1] for three years past."

"Likely enough," said Mr. Princey. "Likely enough. What filth!" He made as if to wipe something off the backs of his hands. "Well, now, we continue. You were in the stable?"

"Yes."

"You were putting the croquet set into its box?"

"Yes."

"You heard someone crossing the yard?"

"Yes."

"It was Withers?"

"Yes."

"So you called him?"

"Yes."

"Loudly? Did you call him loudly? Could anyone have heard?"

"No, Father. I'm sure not. I didn't call him. He saw me as I went to the door. He just waved his hand and came over."

"How *can* I find out from you whether there was anyone about? Whether he *could* have been seen?"

"I'm sure not, Father. I'm quite sure."

"So you both went into the stable?"

"Yes. It was raining hard."

"What did he say?"

"He said 'Hullo, Milly.' And to excuse him coming in the back way, but he'd set out to walk over to Bass Hill."

[1] The name of the local pub.

"Yes."

"And he said, passing the park, he'd seen the house and suddenly thought of me, and he thought he'd just look in for a minute, just to tell me something. He said he was so happy, he wanted me to share it. He'd heard from the Bishop he was to have the vicarage. And it wasn't only that. It meant he could marry. And he began to stutter. And I thought he meant me."

"Don't tell me what you thought. Exactly what he said. Nothing else."

"Well . . . Oh dear!"

"Don't cry. It is a luxury you cannot afford. Tell me."

"He said no. He said it wasn't me. It's Ella Brangwyn-Davies. And he was sorry. And all that. Then he went to go."

"And then?"

"I went mad. He turned his back. I had the winning post of the croquet set in my hand —— "

"Did you shout or scream? I mean, as you hit him?"

"No. I'm sure I didn't."

"Did he? Come on. Tell me."

"No, Father."

"And then?"

"I threw it down. I came straight into the house. That's all. I wish I were dead!"

"And you met none of the servants. No one will go into the stable. You see, George, he probably told people he was going to Bass Hill. Certainly no one knows he came here. He might have been attacked in the woods. We must consider every detail. . . . A curate, with his head battered in —— "

"Don't, Father!" cried Millicent.

"Do you want to be hanged? A curate, with his head battered in, found in the woods. Who'd want to kill Withers?"

There was a tap on the door, which opened immediately. It was little Captain Smollett, who never stood on ceremony. "Who'd kill Withers?" said he. "I would, with pleasure. How d'you do, Mrs. Princey. I walked right in."

"He heard you, Father," moaned Millicent.

"My dear, we can all have our little joke," said her father. "Don't pretend to be shocked. A little theoretical curate-killing, Smollett. In these days we talk nothing but thrillers."

"Parsonicide," said Captain Smollett. "Justifiable parsonicide. Have you heard about Ella Brangwyn-Davies? I shall be laughed at."

"Why?" said Mr. Princey. "Why should you be laughed at?"

"Had a shot in that direction myself," said Smollett, with careful sangfroid. "She half said yes, too. Hadn't you heard? She told most people. Now it'll look as if I got turned down for a white rat in a dog collar."

"Too bad!" said Mr. Princey.

"Fortune of war," said the little captain.

"Sit down," said Mr. Princey. "Mother, Millicent, console Captain Smollett with your best light conversation. George and I have something to look to. We shall be back in a minute or two, Smollett. Come, George."

It was actually five minutes before Mr. Princey and his son returned.

"Excuse me, my dear," said Mr. Princey to his wife. "Smollett, would you care to see something rather interesting? Come out to the stables for a moment."

They went into the stable yard. The buildings were now unused except as odd sheds. No one ever went there. Captain Smollett entered, George followed him, Mr. Princey came last. As he closed the door he took up a gun which stood behind it. "Smollett," said he, "we have come out to shoot a rat which George heard squeaking under that tub. Now, you must listen to me very carefully or you will be shot by accident. I mean that."

Smollett looked at him. "Very well," said he. "Go on."

"A very tragic happening has taken place this afternoon," said Mr. Princey. "It will be even more tragic unless it is smoothed over."

"Oh?" said Smollett.

"You heard me ask," said Mr. Princey, "who would kill Withers. You heard Millicent make a comment, an unguarded comment."

"Well?" said Smollett. "What of it?"

"Very little," said Mr. Princey. "Unless you heard that Withers had met a violent end this very afternoon. And that, my dear Smollett, is what you are going to hear."

"Have you killed him?" cried Smollett.

"Millicent has," said Mr. Princey.

"Hell!" said Smollett.

"It *is* hell," said Mr. Princey. "You would have remembered — and guessed."

"Maybe," said Smollett. "Yes. I suppose I should."

"Therefore," said Mr. Princey, "you constitute a problem."

"Why did she kill him?" said Smollett.

"It is one of these disgusting things," said Mr. Princey. "Pitiable, too. She deluded herself that he was in love with her."

"Oh, of course," said Smollett.

"And he told her about the Brangwyn-Davies girl."

"I see," said Smollett.

"I have no wish," said Mr. Princey, "that she should be proved either a lunatic or a murderess. I could hardly live here after that."

"I suppose not," said Smollett.

"On the other hand," said Mr. Princey, "you know about it."

"Yes," said Smollett. "I am wondering if I could keep my mouth shut. If I promised you —— "

"I am wondering if I could believe you," said Mr. Princey.

"If I promised," said Smollett.

"If things went smoothly," said Mr. Princey. "But not if there was any sort of suspicion, any questioning. You would be afraid of being an accessory."

"I don't know," said Smollett.

"I do," said Mr. Princey. 'What are we going to do?"

"I can't see anything else," said Smollett. "You'd never be fool enough to do me in. You can't get rid of two corpses."

"I regard it," said Mr. Princey, "as a better risk than the other. It could be an accident. Or you and Withers could both disappear. There are possibilities in that."

"Listen," said Smollett. "You can't — "

"Listen," said Mr. Princey. "There may be a way out. There is a way out, Smollett. You gave me the idea yourself."

"Did I?" said Smollett. "What?"

"You said you would kill Withers," said Mr. Princey. "You have a motive."

"I was joking," said Smollett.

"You are always joking," said Mr. Princey. "People think there must be something behind it. Listen, Smollett, I can't trust you, therefore you must trust me. Or I will kill you now, in the next minute. I mean that. You can choose between dying and living."

"Go on," said Smollett.

"There is a sewer here," said Mr. Princey, speaking fast and forcefully. "That is where I am going to put Withers. No outsider knows he has come up here this afternoon. No one will ever look there for him unless you tell them. You must give me evidence that you have murdered Withers."

"Why?" said Smollett.

"So that I shall be dead sure that you will never open your lips on the matter," said Mr. Princey.

"What evidence?" said Smollett.

"George," said Mr. Princey, "hit him in the face, hard."

"Good God!" said Smollett.

"Again," said Mr. Princey. "Don't bruise your knuckles."

"Oh!" said Smollett.

"I'm sorry," said Mr. Princey. "There must be traces of a struggle between you and Withers. Then it will not be altogether safe for you to go to the police."

"Why won't you take my word?" said Smollett.

"I will when we've finished," said Mr. Princey. "George, get that croquet post. Take your handkerchief to it. As I told you, Smollett, you'll just grasp the end of this croquet post. I shall shoot you if you don't."

"Oh, hell," said Smollett. "All right."

"Pull two hairs out of his head, George," said Mr. Princey, "and remember what I told you to do with them. Now, Smollett, you take that bar and raise the big flagstone with the ring in it. Withers is in the next stall. You've got to drag him through and dump him in."

"I won't touch him," said Smollett.

"Stand back, George," said Mr. Princey, raising his gun.

"Wait a minute," cried Smollett. "Wait a minute." He did as he was told.

Mr. Princey wiped his brow. "Look here," said he. "Everything is perfectly safe. Remember, no one knows that Withers came here. Everyone thinks he walked over to Bass Hill. That's five miles of country to search. They'll never look in our sewer. Do you see how safe it is?"

"I suppose it is," said Smollett.

"Now come into the house," said Mr. Princey. "We shall never get that rat."

They went into the house. The maid was bringing tea into the drawing-room. "See, my dear," said Mr. Princey to his wife, "we went to the stable to shoot a rat and we found Captain Smollett. Don't be offended, my dear fellow."

"You must have walked up the back drive," said Mrs. Princey.

"Yes. Yes. That was it," said Smollett in some confusion.

"You've cut your lip," said George, handing him a cup of tea.

"I . . . I just knocked it."

"Shall I tell Bridget to bring some iodine?" said Mrs. Princey. The maid looked up, waiting.

"Don't trouble, please," said Smollett. "It's nothing."

"Very well, Bridget," said Mrs. Princey. "That's all."

"Smollett is very kind," said Mr. Princey. "He knows all our trouble. We can rely on him. We have his word."

"Oh, have we, Captain Smollett?" cried Mrs. Princey. "You *are* good."

"Don't worry, old fellow," Mr. Princey said. "They'll never find anything."

Pretty soon Smollett took his leave. Mrs. Princey pressed his hand very hard. Tears came into her eyes. All three of them watched him go down the drive. Then Mr. Princey spoke very earnestly to his wife for a few minutes and the two of them went upstairs and spoke still more earnestly to Millicent. Soon after, the rain having ceased, Mr. Princey took a stroll round the stable yard.

He came back and went to the telephone. "Put me through to Bass Hill police station," said he. "Quickly . . . Hullo, is that the police station? This is Mr. Princey, of Abbott's Laxton. I'm afraid something rather terrible has happened up here. Can you send someone at once?"

Discussion

1. "Wet Saturday" is a story told largely through the accumulation of detail. In seeking to interpret its meaning, make a list of significant details. Share and discuss your list.

2. Is there a clearly defined beginning, middle, and end in this story? Explain your response. If one of these elements is missing, is its absence justified in terms of the story?

3. This story tells us how some people use others in the pursuit of a goal. What does Mr. Princey seek to achieve and who are the people he uses?

4. Imagine you were one of the villagers who know Mr. Princey only from seeing him on his walks through the village. Com-

pare this impression of him with the one you form of him after reading the story. Discuss why and how the two perspectives change our view of Mr. Princey.

Planning Your Essay Imagine you are a reporter for the village newspaper, which has just been informed that the police have found the body of the curate and have arrested Captain Smollett. You are being sent to get the details of what has happened. Naturally, you will have to decide on your sources of information. You will need to keep in mind that the effectiveness of your account will depend on the order in which you arrange your details. Lastly, you will need to determine when you can get a better effect by writing a sentence in the passive rather than the active and vice versa.

Putting the Essay Together — The Three Stages of Writing You have now reached the point where you are able to put a whole paper together. Your previous writing has consisted primarily of paragraphs of varying lengths: compositions that consolidate into one extended paragraph the introduction, body, or conclusion of an essay; or short one- or two-sentence introductions and conclusions meant to flank a long paragraph. Now you are going to see, step by step, how to write a 500-word expository essay consisting of the introduction, a body consisting of three fully developed paragraphs, and one of the conclusions you have just studied. But, before you embark upon your first assigned 500-word essay, you will probably be interested in some additional suggestions that may ease some of your fears as you venture forth.

The most rewarding experience in writing comes when you feel you have control of almost any writing assignment given you. Although you probably haven't experienced this feeling yet, it will come. Even now, you can make any writing assignment a much easier task if you keep in mind that writing is a process that includes three clearly defined stages. By proceeding through each stage, step by step as delineated below, you can move toward gaining the control you need to discover real joy in writing.

Stage I — The Prewriting Stage

1. Before you put anything on paper, reread your assignment to make sure you understand what you are required to do. Think about the topic you've been assigned. In case you must choose your own topic, be certain that you follow at least one of these requirements:

   a. You know something about the topic.

   b. You are interested in the topic.

   c. You can find some information on it if necessary.

2. Once you have decided on a topic, start thinking about how you intend to approach it. What aspect of the topic are you going to reveal, prove, argue, or dispute? When you have answered this question, you have probably defined your purpose in writing about it. When you can define your purpose, you are ready to formulate your thesis statement.

3. Jot down a few points you intend to make. These are really notes to yourself on your plan of attack, your line of argument.

Stage II — Writing

1. You are now ready to write the first draft of your essay. You have the essentials you need to begin writing — your topic, your thesis statement, and an idea of the main points you are going to make.

2. Writing the first draft is simply a way of getting your ideas down on paper. Here, you cast your thoughts into sentences, organize your sentences into paragraphs. You begin to get the feel of the logical flow of your ideas on the subject as you move from point to point, from general statement to specific support.

3. When you finish the draft, read it through thoughtfully. This is a critical part of the writing process, for now you must make the basic decisions that determine what is going to go into the final draft. You can now revise a sentence, reshape a thought, rethink a point.

4. Write the final draft.

Stage III — Postwriting

1. You have finished the actual writing of your composition. Now may come the toughest part of all, because the temptation is to think that you are finished. You are not. Giving your essay the

critical reading it deserves can often make a significant difference in the amount of praise and approval your essay earns. How many times do you check and recheck with the mirror when you're all dressed up to go out on an important date? Patting your cheek, your hair, straightening your tie, your dress strap, your lapels, your skirt — all these are part of the little ceremonies you engage in to present yourself in the best possible light. Shouldn't you want to present your writing in the best possible light, too?

2. Proofreading is that last-minute grooming you give your written work to make sure that everything is as you want it to be. Among some of the things this reading enables you to spot are:

   a. possible errors in punctuation
   b. subjects and verbs, and nouns and pronouns that don't agree
   c. omitted verb endings, i.e., -ed and -s
   d. spelling errors
   e. errors in tense
   f. sentence fragments

Writing about Your Past or Future   Your major writing effort for this chapter is a 500-word essay in which you attempt to project yourself, say, 10 years from now. Where will you be? What goals and accomplishments do you expect to have realized? What changes will have occurred, or to use a very conventional expression, how much water will have flowed under the bridge?

To help you get started, in fact, to accompany you through each of the various steps of writing this 500-word essay, we give you an example at each step to show how you might develop your own ideas.

In writing your own composition, try to follow as nearly as you can all the steps as they are outlined in the example, moving from prewriting to writing and to the postwriting stage.

Notice that the writer of this sample composition writes from the perspective of 10 years hence and so is looking back at what has happened in the intervening 10 years. You may do the same or, if you prefer, you may write from your present perspective, looking ahead at what you expect to achieve and what you expect to have happen to you.

possible writing assignment

174   Exposition

Writing Your Essay

Step 1　**Thesis statement**
a. Formulate a thesis statement.
b. Since the assignment requires a 500-word essay, you may find it convenient to develop three main points.
c. Let your thesis statement be broad enough to contain the germ of the ideas you will develop.

Example:　In the ten years since I was a student at Hillcrest High, I've learned a lot about life — what winning is, what losing is, and what success really means.

Step 2　**Sketching main points**
Now your task is to generate the three main points that will form the body of your composition. Since this is still the prewriting stage, you can sketch out an outline this way:

Example:　point 1　I achieved some of my goals.
point 2　I learned about failure.
point 3　I discovered something about life.

Step 3　**The introduction**
Now that you know what points you are going to make, you can get down to the actual writing. Naturally, you begin with your introduction. Be sure that your thesis statement includes — and somewhat expands on — the three main points you are going to make.

Example:　Although I'm only twenty-eight now, and from the point of view of some of my friends, that still is a very young age, I believe I've lived and learned a lot. When I was a student at Hillcrest High, I thought life was all goals and accomplishments. I never thought I'd have to know how to accept failure. Nobody ever taught me that. Now, I'm discovering that there is a flow to life, and to be happy you have to jump in the stream and, well, just flow. . . .

Step 4　**Moving into the body of the essay**
Write the first paragraph of the body of your essay. This will cover point 1 of your outline. You may find

it useful to write a topic sentence that states the main point of your paragraph in general terms. Although topic sentences don't necessarily have to be placed at the beginning of every paragraph, they most often are. But wherever your topic sentence appears — at the beginning, the middle, or the end — it is the main sentence, for it states the main idea. Every other sentence in the paragraph flows out of it. (In the following examples, topic sentences are printed in *italics*.)

Example: *Those first few years after graduation, everything went so perfectly well, I couldn't believe it.* I was accomplishing goals left and right. Well, graduation was one. Then on September 21, I got the job I wanted at Youngstown Sheet & Metal Works, in the engineering department. The salary was a dream. Three years after graduation, Sue Ann and I got married. We honeymooned in Acapulco. The trip was a present from our folks.

Step 5 **Developing the body of your essay**
Now, write paragraph 2. Again, lead off with a topic sentence based on the point you wish to make (point 2 of your outline). Follow through with your supporting sentences.

Example: *After that great start, I began to learn about failure, something no one had taught me anything about.* I was doing well on the job — I got a promotion and a raise the first year. Sue Ann and I bought our dream house. All of a sudden, things went wrong. After a long strike, the company let me go as part of the layoff that followed. Even after we sold our car, we couldn't keep up the mortgage payments. Sue Ann had to quit her job because little Al was on the way.

Step 6 **Finishing the body of your essay**
Write paragraph 3 based on point 3. Again, your topic sentence will be your leadoff sentence.

Example: *I began to think I was a failure, a real loser, but what I discovered is that everything is part of life's flow.* This idea floated into my head one day while I was baby-sitting little Al. Sue Ann had gone back to work. I was unemployed. We were living in a two-room apartment. Suddenly, I realized that there's more to life than a timetable for achieving goals. Not long after that, I got a good job. We're happy now. I take things as they come. On most weekends, we go fishing.

Step 7   **Writing the conclusion**
Now you can wind up your essay with your conclusion. It may take one of the five forms suggested earlier in this chapter. Go back and take a look to see which you'd prefer for closing your paper.

Example: In all, these have been 10 great years. I can honestly say I enjoyed all of them, each for different reasons — winning, losing, and learning about life all the while. When I was a student, I might have predicted that some of these things would happen, but certainly not the way they happened. My moral from all this is: Find the stream of life, jump in, and flow with it.

Step 8   **Rewriting**
Steps 1 through 7 have carried you through writing the first draft. After reading it carefully, begin your rewrite. For the steps to follow in the postwriting stage, refer to pp. 173–174.

Checklist for Use before Writing Final Draft

1. Does your essay have an introduction that contains a clear thesis?
2. Does each paragraph of the body focus on one aspect of the thesis?
3. Does your essay conclude with a paragraph that summarizes your thesis and provides a sense of completeness with the help of transitional words or phrases?
4. Have you thoroughly proofread your essay?

Chapter Thirteen

Writing the Process Essay

↗ final assignment

Remember the first time you tried pedalling down the road on your new bike, your father holding the seat from behind, shouting encouragements and instructions and panting as he ran alongside? Or the time you followed your sister's recipe on how to make the perfect French omelet and ended up with dry leathery mishmash that vaguely resembled scrambled eggs from nowhere? And when your friend told you how to get to the new disco joint and you found yourself at the zoo? But then there was the time you followed the directions in the manual and glowed with pride as you heard a voice say "10-4, good buddy" over the CB radio you put together yourself.

Learning how to follow directions is often challenging. It's even more challenging to learn how to give them, particularly in writing since the reader is usually not in a position to ask for clarification when confused. So if you have to write an essay to explain, for example, how the human digestive system works or how to make a 3-dimensional kite, or even how to play chess, you have to explain the steps very clearly and simply. This kind of writing is called *process writing*.

You might wonder what writing a process essay has to do with writing well in school. After all, explaining how to make a kite or play chess is not going to get you an A in your history course, or any other course for that matter. But if you stop and think for a moment, you will realize that assignments for many of the courses you will take in school will require you to write process essays. For a term essay for a business course, for example, you might be asked to explain how to read a balance sheet. In a law course, you might have to write an essay explaining the difference between a provincial law and a federal law. You might be assigned a biology essay requiring an explanation of the workings of the human nervous system.

A very important and handy language tool for writing a process essay is the *transitional word* or *transitional phrase*. Since most processes happen in a time sequence, you should give the reader signals that indicate the order in which a series of actions takes place; this helps avoid confusion. Transitional words or phrases then are helpful in linking a series of instructions or even in keeping ideas in their proper order. Later in this chapter, you will learn what these transitional words are, and how and when to use them.

<u>ACTIVITY</u>   **Writing and Following Directions**   You are now going to take part in an experience that will help you see the importance of clarity, accuracy, and order in describing processes. One activity involves giving directions for getting to a particular place; the other involves instructions for drawing a figure, in other words, for making something.

First, divide into two groups — group A and group B.

Activity for Group A

Leave the classroom. Then, as a group, select a place in the building (for example, the cafeteria, the gym, or the library). Your assignment is to write a set of directions for getting to the place you have selected; later, you will give the directions to group B to follow. Walk toward the chosen place as one member of your group writes down directions for reaching the chosen destination. Once you arrive, find a specific spot and leave a note there for group B. Make sure your directions tell where to find the note. Now return to the classroom, and give the directions to group B.

Activity for Group B

Select one member of your group to draw a simple figure on the chalkboard. Your assignment is to write a set of directions for drawing this figure; afterwards, give the directions to group A to follow. As the artist draws the figure, the rest of you work together on the directions. Have one member of the group copy the figure on a piece of paper.

Both groups then exchange the directions they have worked out, and each group follows the directions of the other group as faithfully as possible. If the directions are clear and simple, group B should return to the classroom with the prize note, and group A should have an accurate reproduction of the figure on the chalkboard. Allow 15 minutes.

Discussion

1. How successful was each group in following through the other group's directions?
2. Which directions of group A were easy to follow? Which were confusing? Why?
3. Which directions of group B were clear enough to follow? Which ones were puzzling? Why?
4. Find some words or phrases in the directions which helped you to know in what order to follow each piece of direction. Do you see a pattern to them?

Whether or not group A or group B was able to follow the other group's directions successfully, both sets of directions were descriptions of a process. When you describe how something functions, how to make or do something, or how to get to a certain place, you are describing a process. A process describes the various stages of action or a series of steps; it is usually controlled by time.

You will have noticed that in explaining what a process is we have often used the word *description*. Do not confuse this kind of description of a technique or method with the kind of description that appeals to the senses. Process writing is directed to the readers' ability to understand and is an appeal to their intellect, not their imagination. It conveys information, not impressions.

IN-CLASS
WRITING

Describing an Action Your teacher will perform an action such as wrapping a package, drinking a glass of water, or putting his or her things together and leaving the room as if the period had ended. Watch carefully and write a paragraph describing step by step, and as accurately and clearly as you can, what your teacher does.

One way of evaluating how completely you described the process is to ask someone else to perform the action as you read your directions aloud to the class. Discuss with your classmates whether the action performed was identical in every detail to the one your teacher performed.

ACTIVITY

Reading Directions The short essay below is a series of directions telling you how to do something, i.e., how to exasperate your English teacher. The time span covered is one class period, and the directions are given in a sequence starting with the beginning of the class period and continuing step by step to the end of the period. As you read it, underline the words that indicate to you the sequential order of each direction.

How to Exasperate Your English Teacher

Did you ever want to drive your English teacher up the wall? Most of us have at one time or another but were afraid to try for fear of the consequences. However, here is an almost foolproof method of doing so without the dire possibilities of being suspended from school or flunking the course.

First, stroll into the class about 10 minutes late. If you walk in earlier the class may not have settled down, and if you're much later, chances are you'll be asked to leave. Next, offer a polite "Good Morning," and continue at the same slow pace across to the far end of the room, seemingly unaware of the loaded, waiting silence. Then sit for a couple of minutes, shifting around restlessly in your seat as the teacher makes an effort to get going. Once he's really into introducing the lesson, get up and walk to a vacant seat as close to him as possible. By now, he's probably ready to ask in a tense, controlled voice why you are disturbing the class. You will explain, again in a polite voice, that you moved because you wished to hear him better. After he makes another attempt to continue with his explanation and you notice the look of absorption creeping back into his eyes, start chatting with your neighbor. However, make sure that the topic of your conversation has to do with the English class. This time you are sure to hear a slight edge in the voice that demands coldly why you insist on distracting everyone. You apologize contritely and let the teacher continue until the explanation is over, and the assignment is given. This relatively lengthy interval will lull his annoyance until, as he looks around at the now silent, busily writing, students, he notices you serenely gazing out the window apparently lost to the world around you.

Now his voice almost cracks with the effort to maintain his composure. You must pretend to start in surprise as you deliberately stumble over an apology and rummage in your bag for pen and paper. Then, raise a trembling hand and whisper out a request for pen and paper, which, you can't understand why, you have forgotten to bring. With cold anger glimmering in his eyes, the teacher will hand you paper and pencil. Let the pencil drop as you reach for it. If you're skillful enough, you will let it fall so as to break its point and the teacher's composure. Five minutes will be taken up in trying to borrow a sharpener or another pencil from one of the distracted students.

By now, there should be approximately 3 to 5 minutes before the bell rings to announce the end of the class period. Sit quietly as if thinking but keep a close watch on the time for the last pitch. Finally, at exactly 30 seconds before time is up, ask in a loud, earnest voice, "Excuse me, Sir, what is the assignment?"

<table>
<tr><td>

**LANGUAGE
LEARNING**

</td><td>

Using Transitional Words Look at the words you have underlined — *first, next, then, after, by now, now, finally.* These words have been used to connect the series of actions in a time sequence. Thus they signal the readers, helping to guide them through the writer's directions. These words are called *transitions.*

</td></tr>
</table>

While the preceding transitions dealt with time, there are other transitions that give different signals without which the connection between two thoughts may not be clear.

Some of the more frequently used transitions give the following signals:

1. Result *therefore, then, thus, hence, consequently, as a result*

> *Example:* (a) Tom worked hard all summer. He was able to pay for a winter vacation in Mexico.
>
> (b) Tom worked hard all summer. *Therefore,* he

was able to pay for a winter vacation in Mexico.

In the version (b) the transition *therefore* makes clear the connection between the first idea and the second.

2. Contrast   *however, on the contrary, nevertheless, on the other hand*

   Example: (a) Hazel was feeling unwell. She decided to go to the party.

   (b) Hazel was feeling unwell. *Nevertheless,* she decided to go to the party.

3. Adding or Amplifying   *in addition, moreover, furthermore, further*

   Example: (a) Marilyn won't speak to me. She won't let her little sister, Jo, talk to me.

   (b) Marilyn won't speak to me. *Moreover,* she won't let her little sister, Jo, talk to me.

4. Time   *sometimes, frequently, often, seldom, never, at the same time, before, after, now, by now, until now*

   Example: (a) Robert and Jim like to see movies. They go to a movie together.

   (b) Robert and Jim like to see movies. *Frequently,* they go together to see a movie.

5. Place   *here, there, above, below, farther on, elsewhere*

   Example: (a) We walked for several kilometres down the road. We saw a yellowish-orange light glowing in the sky.

   (b) We walked for several kilometres. *Farther on* down the road, we saw a yellowish-orange light glowing in the sky.

6. Time sequence   *first, second, next, finally*

   Example: (a) They walked until they were so exhausted they almost collapsed. They came to a little hut where they spent the night.

   (b) They walked until they were so exhausted they almost collapsed. *Finally,* they came to a little hut.

Exercise 1

Write ten pairs of sentences beginning the second sentence with an appropriate transition, from the list above.

Exercise 2

Below are directions for making chicken curry. Underline the transition words in the recipe.

How to Cook Chicken Curry

Most people believe cooking Indian dishes is a complicated and time-consuming process that involves the use of exotic spices with strange names and even stranger smells. However, if you follow the directions below, you will discover that chicken curry, one of the most popular Indian dishes, is a very simple affair.

Get all your ingredients together. For 8 servings, you will need:

16 drumsticks	¼ tsp. cayenne
2 large onions	1 tsp. turmeric
8 cloves fresh garlic	3 cm stick of cinnamon
1 tsp. fresh ginger	6 cardamom seeds
2 Tbsp. coriander powder	1 tsp. whole black pepper
	6 Tbsp. vegetable oil
1 tsp. cumin powder	1 cup plain yogurt

Grate the onions, garlic, and ginger separately. Heat the oil on medium heat until it begins to smoke. When the oil is ready, add the cinnamon stick, cardamom seeds, black pepper, and cloves. Add the grated onions and stir until they are brown. Add the ginger and garlic and stir for about 1 minute. Continue to stir, adding, in order, the coriander powder, cumin powder, cayenne, and turmeric. Keep stirring until the mixture forms a paste and you see oil bubbles seeping through the paste. Add the drumsticks and stir till all pieces are covered with the paste. Cover and let cook for about 10 minutes. While the chicken is cooking, mix 3 cups of water with the cup of yogurt. After 10 minutes are up, pour in the water-and-yogurt mixture, add salt to taste, cover and let cook for about 45 minutes. Garnish with tomato and lemon slices and fresh green parsley or coriander sprigs.

BEATING WRITER'S BLOCK — How to Confront the Typewriter Fearlessly

9:03 a.m. As every schoolboy knows, writer's block is an affliction every bit as debilitating as . . . (*Well, as what? Maybe a cup of coffee will help.*)

Writer's block is a condition that . . .

(*Retrieve paper airplanes, empty wastebasket, reread* Playboy *centerfold. Remember the writer who set fire to his apartment to avoid meeting a deadline?*)

9:25 a.m. (*Try to beat the block by leading off with other people's quotes.*) "Blocks are simply forms of egotism," said Lawrence Durrell . . .

10:32 a.m. (*Maybe this will do it.*) What can be done to break writer's block? There are many traditional answers: change of scenery, change of work habits, drop everything and see a James Bond movie. Durrell recommends insulting oneself while shaving and concentrating on unpaid bills. T.S. Eliot broke his block by writing poems in French. (*Dabbling in lesser languages removes pressure to perform in mother tongue.*) Tom Wolfe, totally blocked on his first famous article, a story about customized cars for *Esquire*, wrote a really socko memorandum to his editor on the subject. The editor ran the memo as the article. Wolfe now writes all his articles as memos. (*On the other hand he is at least three years late with his current book . . .*)

11:09 a.m. Los Angeles Psychoanalyst Martin Grotjahn thinks he knows the cause of the malady. Says he: "People who have strong needs to love or fight are more prone to writer's block." Most psychiatrists believe that, just as there is no single explanation for murder or theft, there is no one cause for writer's block. But Grotjahn, who discusses the problem in his book *Beyond Laughter*, believes hostility is the fundamental reason. Writing is an aggressive demand for attention. It can be blocked when a writer projects his anger onto reviewers and readers. "It's the fear of being attacked," says Manhattan Psychoanalyst Walter Stewart, "the fear that you will be treated as contemptuously as you would like to treat everyone else."

In fact, Herman Melville was so wounded by critics that

he wrote no fiction at all for 30 years. Says Psychoanalyst Yale Kramer, who is studying Melville's life: "He behaved like a child stubbornly remaining silent in a passive attempt at revenge." But even good reviews can bring on writer's block; they tend to paralyze by awakening great expectations. As Author Cyril Connolly, a part-time blockee, expressed it: "Whom the gods wish to destroy they first call promising."

12:15 p.m. (*Word count so far: 385.*) Short break for inner movie about receiving Nobel Prize for literature. Psychiatrists call this the "grandiose fantasy." This imaginary acclaim is a neurotic compromise between the real self — scared, limited — and the ideal self — a literary conqueror. Says Manhattan Analyst Donald Kaplan: "The fantasy of playing Carnegie Hall may be so gratifying that you can't manage to practice your scales."

This is not to be confused with what Kaplan calls "the Nobel Prize complex" — a compulsive perfectionism that drives the writer to type the opening line of a book 403 times. Every word has to be as good as Shakespeare or Shaw, or there is no use playing the game at all. A subvariation, of course, is that it also has to be perfectly typed. Psychoanalyst Edmund Bergler, a brilliant but erratic writer on the 1950s, has a scatological interpretation of the first-line problem: the writer smearing the empty page with words is the baby smearing mommy's living room wall with diaper residue. Bergler, much admired for his own literary wall smearing, churned out a dozen popular books on psychiatry, all of them arguing that masochism explained *most* of human affairs. He could have used a block or two himself.

1:30 p.m. (*Time to lapse into coherence.*) The opposite of the "first-line" problem is the "last-lap paralysis." One screenwriter wrote two-thirds of a script and made the mistake of showing it to friends, who said it was the greatest property ever to hit Hollywood, thus immobilizing the writer.

Fear of success comes in here. One symptom is short sentences. Fear makes you lose your rhythm and forget how English sentences run. (*Bathroom break, check mail.*) But psychiatrists know that the plucky writer can pull up his socks and finish everything he begi

Discussion

1. What is the main point of the article?
2. How is the article organized?
3. Why does the writer insert part of the article in parenthesis?
4. Have you had a similar experience? When?

WHEN YOU CAMP OUT, DO IT RIGHT — Ernest Hemingway

Outside of insects and bum sleeping the rock that wrecks most camping trips is cooking. The average tyro's idea of cooking is to fry everything and fry it good and plenty. Now, a frying pan is a most necessary thing to any trip, but you also need the old stew kettle and the folding reflector baker.

A pan of fried trout can't be bettered and they don't cost any more than ever. But there is a good and bad way of frying them.

The beginner puts his trout and his bacon in and over a brightly burning fire the bacon curls up and dries into a dry tasteless cinder and the trout is burned outside while it is still raw inside. He eats them and it is all right if he is only out for the day and going home to a good meal at night. But if he is going to face more trout and bacon the next morning and other equally well-cooked dishes for the remainder of two weeks he is on the pathway to nervous dyspepsia.

The proper way is to cook over coals. Have several cans of Crisco or Cotosuet or one of the vegetable shortenings along that are as good as lard and excellent for all kinds of shortening. Put the bacon in and when it is about half cooked lay the trout in the hot grease, dipping them in corn meal first. Then put the bacon on top of the trout and it will baste them as it slowly cooks.

The coffee can be boiling at the same time and in a smaller skillet pancakes being made that are satisfying the other campers while they are waiting for the trout.

With the prepared pancake flours you take a cupful of pancake flour and add a cup of water. Mix the water and flour and as soon as the lumps are out it is ready for cooking. Have the skillet hot and keep it well greased. Drop the batter in and as soon as it is done on one side loosen it in the skillet and flip it over. Apple butter, syrup or cinnamon and sugar go well with the cakes.

While the crowd have taken the edge from their appetites with flapjacks the trout have been cooked and they and the bacon are ready to serve. The trout are crisp outside and firm and pink inside and the bacon is well done — but not too done. If there is anything better than that combination the writer has yet to taste it in a lifetime devoted largely and studiously to eating.

The stew kettle will cook you dried apricots when they have resumed their predried plumpness after a night of soaking, it will serve to concoct a mulligan in, and it will cook macaroni. When you are not using it, it should be boiling water for the dishes.

In the baker, mere man comes into his own, for he can make a pie that to his bush appetite will have it all over the product that mother used to make, like a tent. Men have always believed that there was something mysterious and difficult about making a pie. Here is a great secret. There is nothing to it. We've been kidded for years. Any man of average office intelligence can make at least as good a pie as his wife.

All there is to a pie is a cup and a half of flour, one-half teaspoonful of salt, one-half cup of lard and cold water. That will make pie crust that will bring tears of joy into your camping partner's eyes.

Mix the salt with the flour, work the lard into the flour, make it up into a good workmanlike dough with cold water. Spread some flour on the back of a box or something flat, and pat the dough around a while. Then roll it out with whatever kind of round bottle you prefer. Put a little more lard on the surface of the sheet of dough and then slosh a little flour on and roll it up and then roll it out again with the bottle.

Cut out a piece of the rolled out dough big enough to line a pie tin. I like the kind with holes in the bottom. Then put in your dried apples that have soaked all night and been sweetened, or your apricots, or your blueberries, and then take another sheet of the dough and drape it gracefully over the top, soldering it down at the edges with your fingers. Cut a couple of slits in the top dough sheet and prick it a few times with a fork in an artistic manner.

Put it in the baker with a good slow fire for forty-five minutes and then take it out and if your pals are Frenchmen they will kiss you. The penalty for knowing how to cook is that the others will make you do all the cooking.

It is all right to talk about roughing it in the woods. But the real woodsman is the man who can be really comfortable in the bush.

Discussion

1. What is the main point of the piece?
2. What method does Hemingway use to expand his main idea?
3. How many preparations does he describe through his method?
4. Since the process described here is cooking a meal, very few transitions are used. Can you recognize them? What kind of transitions are they?

FORMAL WRITING

Describing How to Keep or Break a Friendship In this chapter, you have learned about writing a clear and accurate process paper, and you have learned to use transitions to help make the sequential order of the process understandable. However, as you recognized from the readings above, a process essay, like any other essay, must also have an introduction which includes the main idea or thesis; a body, which in this case includes the description of a process; and a conclusion, which restates the main idea and sums up the supporting points of your essay.

Write an essay on one of the two topics below:

Topic 1 How to meet someone, how to make friends with that person, and how to sustain the friendship

Topic 2 How to recognize a bad friend, how to break the friendship, and how to keep it broken

Remember to use transitions not only concerning time, but also those that signal results, contrast, addition, and conclusion. However, be careful to use them only when they help to clarify the connection between two sentences. In other words, do not start every sentence with a transition.

Checklist for Use before Writing Final Draft

1. Does your essay have: a) an introduction with a thesis; b) a body, explaining the three aspects in a logical and interesting manner; and c) a conclusion that sums up the essay and gives a sense of completion?
2. Did you use transitions when necessary?
3. Have you proofread your essay for sentence variety? Is your writing vivid? Are your pronouns complete and correct?

Chapter Fourteen

Writing the Comparison and Contrast Essay

Often in writing you will be asked to deal with several ideas, places, persons, situations, or things. You might, for example, have to write about two approaches to physical fitness, the main characters in two short stories, the three candidates for mayor, a traditional and an innovative design for an elementary-school classroom, or a particular approach to alcoholism and its relationship to programs for alcoholics in your town. In these essays, you will probably want first to discuss the similarities and differences between the different things you are writing about, and then to conclude which is better or more useful or to propose a viable combination of the best aspects of each. Expository essays that show how ideas, people, places, things, or situations are similar and how they differ are called *comparison-contrasts*. Such an essay, like the others you have been learning about, has an introduction with a thesis, a body of several paragraphs that develop your ideas, and a conclusion, which summarizes the main points. In comparison-contrast essays, though, there are different ways to organize the body. This chapter will present those approaches.

You have been comparing and contrasting things all your life. When you were 5 and you chose to play with the dump truck instead of the blocks, or when you were 14 and you chose to go to Burger King instead of McDonald's, you were reaching your decisions almost unconsciously by comparing and contrasting. It is very natural to recognize similarities and differences and then on these bases to determine what suits you best at that moment. You also use the process frequently to convince someone of something. Remember when your father didn't want to leave you home over the weekend while he and your mother were away because of what happened the last time they left you alone? You explained to your parents that you had changed and that they could now rely on you. You compared and contrasted the way you are today with the way you were then in order to convince them of your trustworthiness.

Comparing and contrasting are useful in decision-making, explaining, understanding, and convincing. You rely on the process often in your daily lives, and you will have considerable use for it during your academic career. In this chapter, you will learn to write well-organized comparison-contrast essays.

ACTIVITY **Planning Improvements in Your Community** More than likely your community developed haphazardly. Of course, haphazardness has a style to it here in North America. Many small Canadian towns have, for example, a center with stores and public facilities and a highway with a shopping center. If you lived in town, you probably had a small backyard to play in, sidewalks to run on, and stores nearby to shop in. If you lived out of town, you had to have an adult drive you everywhere when you were a child; when you were old enough, you may have gotten a bike so you could roam around by yourself; you always had plenty of countryside to have adventures in. Canadian cities have stores and public facilities in their downtowns, uptowns, and midtowns; people live all over and have buses and often subways to get them where they want to go. But greenery is limited, and most adventures take place on the sidewalks. There are good and bad things about life in the cities and about life in the small towns. What community planners attempt to do is create cities that consider the needs of people and contribute to the individual's sense of well-being. Today you will have an opportunity to try your hand at community planning.

This activity involves developing plans to improve a community, town, or city that is of concern to your class. If the plans you develop are worthwhile, you might actually want to submit them to a local planning board, but for now they are for class use.

Divide into four groups. Group 1 will be the planning board. It will consist of three class members whose role will be to award a $30-million grant to the best plan to improve the community. The rest of the class will form groups 2, 3, and 4. Each will write a community-improvement proposal, competing to win the $30-million grant.

Look at the list below. It includes items that might call for improvement or change, depending on the community your class has decided to develop plans for. You may focus your proposal on any combination of these items.

Housing
multiple dwellings
single-family dwellings
housing for the elderly
housing for the handicapped
lower-, middle-, and upper-income housing
economically, racially, and ethnically integrated housing

Industry and Commerce
development of industry
pollution control
transportation
jobs
job training
stores
commercial areas

Public Services
health
  hospitals
  clinics
  preventive services
education
  elementary schools
  junior high schools
  senior high schools
  colleges
  graduate schools
  adult education
  job training
  senior-citizens programs
  handicapped programs

physical-fitness programs
reading-skills programs
recreation
  parks
  beaches
  sports facilities
  entertainment facilities
  cultural developments and facilities
  theatre
  music
  art
  dance
libraries
environmental services
  sanitation
  pollution control
  beautification
transportation
  buses
  subways
  parking
  bike paths
  road maintenance
  highways
  sidewalks
emergency services
  police
  fire
  ambulance

Group Instructions

This activity involves decision-making. To arrive at decisions, you must compare and contrast. You must look at the community you have selected and determine what its strengths and its weaknesses are. To help you do this efficiently, look back at the list above and on the previous page.

An examination of your community may reveal that housing facilities need improvement, that the downtown area is falling apart, and that public facilities need to be upgraded. You may decide that the way to get the most for your money, though, is to improve housing. Perhaps your examination revealed a shortage of housing facilities for middle-income individuals and families. You may also have noted that housing for lower-income families is in poor condition. Therefore your proposal for the $30 million will be to improve housing; the proposal might call for 25 percent of the money to upgrade already existing housing, 50 percent of the money to build multiple dwellings that would integrate lower- and middle-income individuals and families, and 25 percent of the money to build new single-family dwellings for middle-income families. You might justify this plan first by indicating that steps to keep middle-income individuals and families in the area could increase the area's tax revenue, thereby providing increased resources for public services and for upgrading the downtown area. Second, you could point out that upgrading housing for lower-income individuals and families is a humane necessity. Finally, you could show that integrating these economic groups could improve the tense social relations that currently exist in your community. To come up with valid proposals, you must look at what already exists and determine what is needed; you must also supply reasons why your plan should be put into effect.

Planning Board

To prepare for the decisions you will have to make when choosing the best of the proposals, do the following:

1. Look over the items in the three categories listed on p. 192 and determine among yourselves which aspects your area is strong in and which aspects need improvement. Spend some time talking over what areas you hope groups 2, 3, and 4 will propose.
2. Now rank the areas. If you decide that housing for the elderly is most urgent, rank it number 1. If you believe pollution control is essential in your area but not as crucial as housing for the elderly, rank it number 2. Rank all of the items on the list which need to be improved. By doing this, you will have some basis on which to make your decisions when the other groups submit their proposals.
3. Listen to each group's proposal for community improvement. Compare their priorities with your own. Ask any questions you need to. Decide which proposal offers the most to satisfy the needs of your community. Either award the $30 million to a single group or divide the money among them as you see fit.

Groups 2, 3, and 4

Step 1 Eliminate those items from the list that the community, town, or city adequately provides.

Step 2 Select the areas that need improvement.

Step 3 Decide which aspects you will include in your plan, what should be done to improve them, and how much money (what percentage of the $30 million) should be spent on these improvements.

Step 4 Draft your plan.

Step 5 Write up an explanation of the value of your plan; show what it will improve and why this improvement is vital.

Step 6 Revise your plan. Have one member of the group read the plan to the rest of the group. Listen to one another's suggestions and make any changes that will strengthen your plan and your chances of winning the $30-million grant for enacting your plan.

Step 7 Present your finished plan and your justification for it to the planning board.

Discussion

1. Look at the plans or the parts of the plans that were awarded funds. Why were these plans best?
2. During this activity, you did a lot of comparing and contrasting. List on the board all the instances when you used comparisons or contrasts. What purposes did the use of these serve?
3. In what instances are comparisons and contrast useful?

READINGS

Writings that point out similarities are called *comparisons;* writings that make the reader aware of differences are called *contrasts.* When you write a paper that compares, contrasts, or does both, there are two different patterns you can use to organize your information. The readings that follow are similar in content but differ in organization. When you read them, compare and contrast them.

THE COURTSHIP OF ARTHUR AND AL — James Thurber

Once upon a time there was a young beaver named Al and an older beaver named Arthur. They were both in love with a pretty little female. She looked with disfavor upon the young beaver's suit because he was a harum-scarum and a ne'er-do-well. He had never done a single gnaw of work in his life, for he preferred to eat and sleep and to swim lazily in the streams and to play Now-I'll-Chase-You with the girls. The older beaver had never done anything but work from the time he got his first teeth. He had never played anything with anybody.

When the young beaver asked the female to marry him, she said she wouldn't think of it unless he amounted to something. She reminded him that Arthur had built thirty-two dams and was working on three others, whereas he, Al, had never even made a bread-board or a pin tray in his life. Al was very sorry, but he said he would never go to work just because a woman wanted him to. Thereupon she offered to be a sister to him, but he pointed out that he already had seventeen sisters. So he went back to eating and sleeping and swimming in the streams and playing Spider-in-the-Parlor with the girls. The female married Arthur one day at the lunch hour — he could never get away from work for more than one hour at a time. They had seven children and Arthur worked so hard supporting them he wore his teeth down to the gum line. His health broke in two before long and he died without ever having had a vacation in his life. The young beaver continued to eat and sleep and swim in the streams and play Unbutton-Your-Shoe with the girls. He never Got Anywhere, but he had a long life and a Wonderful Time.

MORAL: It is better to have loafed and lost than never to have loafed at all.

ARTHUR AND AL, RETOLD

Once upon a time there were two beavers named Al and Arthur. They were both in love with a pretty little female.

Al was a young beaver. The pretty little female looked with disfavor upon his suit because he was a harum-scarum and ne'er-do-well. He had never done a single gnaw of work in his life, for he preferred to eat and sleep and to swim lazily in the streams and to play Now-I'll-Chase-You with the girls. When Al asked the pretty little female to marry him, she said she wouldn't think of it unless he amounted to something. He had not even made a bread-board or a pin tray in his life. Al was very sorry, but he said he would never go to work just because a woman wanted him to. Thereupon, she offered to be a sister to him, but he pointed out that he already had seventeen sisters. So he went back to eating and sleeping and swimming in the streams and playing Spider-in-the-Parlor with the girls.

Arthur was the older beaver. He had never done anything but work from the time he got his first teeth. He had never played anything with anybody. The pretty little female looked upon Arthur with favor because he had built thirty-two dams and was working on three others. So she married him one fine day at the lunch hour — he could never get away from work for more than one hour at a time. They had seven children and Arthur worked so hard supporting them, he wore his teeth down to the gum line. Arthur's health broke in two before long and he died without ever having had a vacation in his life. Al continued to eat and sleep and swim in the streams and play Unbutton-Your-Shoe with the girls. He never Got Anywhere, but he had a long life and a Wonderful Time.

MORAL: It is better to have loafed and lost than never to have loafed at all.

Discussion

1. In what ways are the two selections similar? How do they differ?
2. What is the pattern of organization used in the first selection? What is it in the second?

Organizing the Comparison and Contrast Essay

Point-by-Point Organization

In the story as told by Thurber, the characteristics of Arthur and Al are compared and contrasted point by point. As each aspect of the event is told, both Arthur and Al are discussed. You first learn that both beavers love the same "pretty little female." You then read about their very different life-styles, about Arthur, the hardworker, and Al, the playful ne'er-do-well. Next you find out what happens to their marriage proposals, and finally you are told that later on in life Arthur, toothless and joyless, dies, while

Al, who "never got anywhere," has a "long life and a wonderful time."

A picture of this point by point comparison contrast looks like this:

Introduction   2 Beavers Named Al and Arthur

Body
Circumstances: Al loves the pretty little female.
Arthur loves the pretty little female.
Life-style: Al is a playful ne'er-do-well.
Arthur is a hard worker.
Proposal: Al's marriage proposal is rejected.
Arthur marries the pretty little female.
Later life: Arthur works hard, loses his health, dies young.
Al continues to play, lives long, and has a wonderful time.
Conclusion: It is better to have loafed and lost than never to have loafed at all.

Block Organization

In the second version of the piece, the information is organized in blocks. The body consists of two paragraphs, the first of which tells everything about Al, and the second of which tells all about Arthur.

A picture of this method of organizing the comparison-contrast looks like this:

Introduction   Arthur and Al love a pretty little female.

Body
Al: 1. Ne'er-do-well, playful life-style.
2. His marriage proposal is rejected.
Arthur: 1. Hard worker.
2. Marries the pretty little female.

Conclusion   Arthur dies.
Al lives.
It is better to have loafed and lost than never to have loafed at all.

When you write essays that include or consist entirely of comparison and/or contrast, you will have to decide which pattern of organization — the point-by-point pattern or the block pattern — is best. The nature of the information you are comparing or contrasting and the purpose of your essay, your thesis, will affect your decision.

IN-CLASS
WRITING **Writing Your Own Fable** Below are several well-known proverbs. Select one proverb and write a fable in which you use comparison and contrast to support it. You may use the proverb as stated or, like Thurber, you can change it around. Once you select the information you will include to support the proverb, look it over and select the organization pattern that seems most appropriate.

Proverbs

1. Early to bed and early to rise
   makes a man healthy, wealthy, and wise.
2. Too many cooks spoil the broth.
3. A stitch in time saves nine.
4. A bird in hand is worth two in the bush.
5. Better late than never.
6. The early bird catches the worm.
7. Honesty is the best policy.
8. 'Tis better to have loved and lost
   than never to have loved at all.

Change the proverb if you wish.

ACTIVITY **Comparing Photos of Activity** On pp. 200 and 201 are two pictures, taken at different times. However, the nature of the scene has changed substantially in the time frame that has elapsed between the two photographs.

Look at each photograph carefully and then make a list of everything you see in each one, as shown below.

Picture A   *Picture B*

_____   _____
_____   _____
_____   _____
_____   _____

200 *Exposition*

When you have finished, compare your lists with your fellow students'. Add any details they have that you may have omitted.

In completing your lists you have taken the first step toward writing a comparison-contrast paper. Using the block method of organization, you would have a paragraph describing the main features of the area as it appeared in the 1900s and a second paragraph noting the similarities and differences in the 1930s. However, you also need a statement that provides a focus for your comparison. What do you feel is the nature of the change that has occurred? Your answer to that question will provide the controlling idea for your comparison, just as the proverbs suggested as morals for the in-class writing provided the main idea for your fables. Reread your lists and select the eight or ten details that best prove your thesis and make two lists, like those below.

Thesis: _____ .

Picture A   Picture B

_____   _____

_____   _____

_____   _____

_____   _____

Now you will reorganize your material to prepare a paper using point-by-point organization. Look over your original lists for each of the pictures and see what categories of details you can isolate. You will probably have one on the differences in the buildings you see, another on the kinds of transportation shown, and a third on the activities. Using the same thesis, regroup your material into three paragraphs each of which discusses a different category.

Thesis: _____

Category 1: _____

      Picture A _____

_____

      Picture B _____

_____

Category 2: _____

    Picture A _____

_____

    Picture B _____

_____

Category 3: _____

    Picture A _____

_____

    Picture B _____

_____

FORMAL WRITING

Writing about Your City Now and in the Future Much of the material presented in this chapter has centered on where and how one lives, and on the kinds of changes people and time can effect on the profile of a city or town. The activity at the beginning of the chapter asked you to become a city planner who has a voice in the kinds of changes the city or town where you live undergoes.

When you studied the changes that occurred in Times Square over a period of approximately 30 years, you saw many kinds of changes. Unfortunately, you have no way of knowing how many of those changes were planned, or whether they were ultimately good or bad for the people who lived and worked there. For whatever purpose, and no matter to whose advantage or disadvantage, the changes did occur.

Now take a look at the city or town where you live. Look at it critically; consider the possibilities for improvement and change that would benefit all its inhabitants. Select three important aspects that you believe will make it a more humanly livable city or town. Project what you would like to see in 20 years. Because this is a comparison-contrast paper, you will have to decide the best way of moving clearly from point to point.

Checklist for Use before Writing Final Draft

1. Do you have a thesis in your introduction?
2. Have you used comparison and contrast to emphasize your thesis?
3. Which method of organization did you use?
4. Does your conclusion reinforce your thesis?
5. Have you carefully proofread your essay?

Afterword

Whether you thought it would ever happen or not, it has. You have finally reached the end of this book. You might like to take a moment or two here to consider the distance you have travelled as a writer and to think over where things began to fall into place along the way. Somewhere along the path this book has forged for you, did an awareness emerge that made you feel you were becoming a competent writer?

You may even want to take out some of the assignments you did and arrange them in the order in which they occurred in this book. As you do this, look at your teacher's comments to see if they reflect something that was beginning to happen in you. Maybe they are telling you that writing well is neither a mystery nor an accident. You can actually make it happen whenever you wish. Your growing ability as a writer may have come about without your having realized it. We think you should know if it has happened.

Finally, as you look at yourself as a writer, remember that writing is an experience, and since it is, you ought to feel as good about it as possible. This good feeling is best defined as confidence. From page 1, the goal of our book has been to help you develop that confidence in you. As you move into more advanced writing courses, you will experience further growth and greater confidence. Accept our best wishes. We are confident of your success.

The Authors

Appendix

Spelling   One of the first problems that will face you as you begin serious writing is the problem of spelling. A dictionary (perhaps a special one for those with spelling difficulties), a notebook in which to write down the words you do not know, and a few minutes a day to study them — these will help you overcome the most serious of your spelling errors.

There are a group of words, however, that may cause confusion. These are words that are pronounced the same but not spelled the same. Because these words mean very different things, you can cause misunderstandings unless you use the correct one.

To Apostrophe or Not to Apostrophe

One of the major uses of the apostrophe (') is to indicate that a letter has been left out. You can use an apostrophe to change *do not* into *don't*. Here the apostrophe takes the place of the omitted *o*. In some cases, if you forget to put it in, you will create confusing sentences.

1. It's/its   In the word *it's*, the apostrophe takes the place of the omitted letter *i* of *it is*, or the omitted letters *ha* of *has*. *It's* = *it is* or *it has*. Those are the only meanings it can have.

Examples: *It's* not easy to learn to spell. (*It is* not easy to learn to spell.)

It's been difficult finding a job. (*It has* been difficult finding a job.)

Problem: The word *its* (without the apostrophe) has a completely different meaning. It is used to show ownership.

Examples: The country faced *its* problems with courage. The art museum brought *its* pictures to the community.

Test yourself: If you can substitute *it is* or *it has*, you need the apostrophe.

    If the subject and verb of your sentence (if you do not know these terms, read the explanation in Chapter 3) are *it* and *is* or *has*, you need the apostrophe.

    Write five sentences using *it's*. Write each sentence twice. The second time use *it is* or *it has* instead of *it's*.

2. You're/your The apostrophe in *you're* takes the place of the *a* in the word *are*, so *you're* = *you are*.

Example: *You're* going to be late for work if you don't leave now. (*You are* going to be. . . .)

Problem: Your (without the apostrophe) shows ownership.

Example: You will forget *your* books if you leave them under the chair.

Test yourself: If you can substitute *you are*, you need the apostrophe.

    If the subject and verb of your sentence are *you* and *are*, you need the apostrophe.

    If the word that follows is the name of a person, place, or thing, you usually need *your* (no apostrophe).

    Write five sentences using *you're*. Write each sentence twice. The second time use *you are* instead of *you're*.

3. Who's/whose The apostrophe takes the place of the *i* in *who is*, so *who's* = *who is*. That is its only meaning.

Example: *Who's* going to the dance tonight? (*Who is* going to the dance tonight?)

Problem: Whose (without the apostrophe) shows ownership.

Example: *Whose* book is on the window ledge?

Test yourself: If you can substitute *who is*, you need the form with the apostrophe.

If the subject and verb of your sentence or clause are *who* and *is*, you need the apostrophe.

If the word that follows is the name of a person, place or thing, you usually need *whose* (no apostrophe).

Write five sentences using *who's*. Write each sentence twice. The second time use *who is* instead of *who's*.

4. They're/their/there The apostrophe in *they're* takes the place of the *a* in *are*, so *they're* = *they are*.

Example: They're going to the dance tonight.

(*They are* going to the dance tonight.)

Problem: There indicates a place or is used in an opening phrase, while *their* shows ownership.

Examples: Joe left his gloves over *there*.

There are three reasons why I cannot go.

The girls brought *their* problems to *their* counselor.

(We will discuss the differences between *their* and *there* more fully later in this section.)

Test yourself: If you can substitute *they are*, you need the form with the apostrophe. Be sure you don't mean *there are* because you can't use an apostrophe in that phrase.

If the subject and verb of your sentence are *they* and *are*, you need the apostrophe.

Write five sentences using *they're*. Write each sentence twice. The second time use *they are*.

Exercise
Read the following selection and fill in the blanks, using *it's* or *its*; *you're* or *your*; *who's* or *whose*; *they're*, *their*, or *there are*, as appropriate.

The basketball team is having problems. _____ going to carry the equipment to the game? Bob and Joe think _____ too busy to do that, but Dick and Mike think _____ not _____ responsibility. Dick told Joe, "_____ not any busier than I am. You ought to do _____ share of the work." But Bob said, "_____ a simple matter of sharing the work. _____ car do we use? If we use mine, then I shouldn't have to carry the balls and stuff." "Yeah," replied Dick, "but if _____ tire goes flat, _____ supposed to fix it?"

Sound-Alikes That Don't Look Alike

1. Two/To/Too   These tiny words cause very big problems.

Two: *Two = 2.* If you are counting a number of items, this is the spelling you want.

Example: I had *two* apples and Jane had *two* pears.

To: *Indicating direction.* If you want to tell where someone or something went, you need *to.*

Example: Betty went *to* church every Sunday.

Before a verb (action word). When you want the word that goes before a verb, you want *to.* (*To* plus the verb is called an infinitive.)

Example: *To succeed* in school, you have *to work.*

Too: If you mean *more than enough* or *very,* you need *too.* If you mean *also,* you need *too.*

Examples: Tracy is *too* busy to help us.
Will you read your essay to the class, *too?*

Test yourself: Determine which of these meanings you want; then check the spelling for that meaning.
Check to see if the word that follows is a verb (action word); if so, use *to.*
Check to see if you mean *more than enough;* if so, use *too.* (Hint: *Too* has more than enough o's.)

2. Where/were   These words should be pronounced somewhat differently. *Where* rhymes with *hair; were* rhymes with *purr;* but sometimes the two are confused.
Where tells us *at what place.*

Example: *Where* did you leave your surfboard?

Were indicates the action or part of the action of the sentence. It is a verb.

Example: The boys *were* working on the car.

The girls *were* happy.

Test yourself: If you mean *at what place*, use *where*.

If you are giving the verb in the sentence, use *were*. Note that when you use *were*, you should be talking about the past.

Exercise

Fill in the blanks with the words *where, were, two, to,* and *too* as appropriate.

Mary and I decided _____ bake a cake. We needed _____ eggs, so I went to the refrigerator _____ I found the egg box. We _____ about to crack the shells when Mary screamed, "We forgot _____ turn on the oven!" I was so surprised I dropped an egg on the floor. The _____ of us _____ laughing so hard the tears came _____ our eyes.

Write five sentences for each of the forms we have been discussing.

3. There/their (they're) We already talked about this group when dealing with apostrophes, so you already know that *they're* can only mean *they are. There* refers to place.

Example: I left the basketball over *there*, by the water fountain.

There is also used as part of opening phrases.

Example: There are three main causes of the Civil War.

Their shows ownership.

Example: The boys left *their* jackets on the grass.

Test yourself: If you can substitute the names of two or more people (for example, Dick and Jane) for the needed word, you should use *their*.

If there is a verb (usually *is* or *are*) immediately following the word, you should use *there*.

Note that if you take the *t* off of *there*, you have *here*, so you know it refers to place.

Exercise

Write five sentences using the forms we have been discussing.

There are a number of other confusing sound-alikes —
*then/than, rode/road, led/lead, piece/peace, lose/loose,
knew/new, dye/die, know/no.* If you have trouble with any of
these, look them up in the dictionary and write your own definitions. Then write sentences for each of them.

MORE
WORK
ON
MODIFIERS
AND
MODIFYING
PHRASES

Basic Sentence Structure   This section gives you more practice with modifiers and reinforces your understanding of basic
sentence structure.

Modifiers add life to sentences. Although a subject and a verb
are the basic core of the sentence, they do not by themselves make
for very exciting reading. Few people would be content with a
steady fare of two- and three-word sentences. The precision and
complexity of mature thinking require precise and complex sentences.

One of the simplest ways to expand your sentences is by adding modifying words and phrases, which can transform dull,
vague sentences into ones that are both vivid and specific.

Example: The man laughed.

The *broad, dark* man with the *thick walrus mus-
tache laughed scornfully.*

Modifying Words

1. Descriptive words can be placed in front of a noun. Words
that indicate, for instance, size, shape, color, or texture help the
reader to sense the person or object. Usually two or three such
words are enough; only in exceptional cases would you want to
use more.

Example: A *slimy green* snake slithered by.

Add modifiers as indicated to the following sentences:

1. The ———— apple fell to the ground. (color, texture)
2. The ———— bird sang. (size, color)
3. The ———— grass swayed. (size, color)
4. The ———— girl climbed the tree. (shape, size)

When you have finished, circle the subject-verb core for each
sentence.

2. Descriptive words can be used to tell how an action was performed. These words, often ending in *-ly,* give your reader a better grasp of your meaning.

Example: The small green Vega swerved *dangerously.*

Exercise
Add modifiers to both the subject and the verb in the following sentences:

1. The ＿＿＿＿ dog yelped ＿＿＿＿.
2. The ＿＿＿＿ girl peered ＿＿＿＿.
3. The ＿＿＿＿ house burned ＿＿＿＿.
4. The ＿＿＿＿ newspaper blew ＿＿＿＿.

When you have finished, circle the subject-verb core of each sentence.

Modifying Phrases — Description

Phrases can be used to add additional descriptive details and are especially helpful when you have already used a few modifying words in front of a noun subject.

Example: The lean, grey dog *with the long thick tail* sniffed warily.

Exercise
Add a modifying phrase as well as modifiers to both the subject and the verb in the following sentences.

1. The ＿＿＿＿ boy with ＿＿＿＿ sang ＿＿＿＿.
2. The ＿＿＿＿ cat with ＿＿＿＿ played ＿＿＿＿ in the yard.
3. The ＿＿＿＿ bridge with ＿＿＿＿ swayed ＿＿＿＿ in the storm.
4. The ＿＿＿＿ kettle with ＿＿＿＿ whistled ＿＿＿＿ on the stove.

Notice that the subject-verb core has been divided by the modifying phrase in the above sentences. Circle the subject and verb in each sentence and draw a line to connect the circles.

Modifying Phrases — Adding Detail

Phrases can also add details that make your meaning more specific. By using phrases that begin with *in, at, under, behind, through, of,* etc., you can add a great deal of valuable information.

Much of this information supplies answers to questions such as **where?** (*at the store, under the table*); **when?** (*in a few minutes, by tomorrow afternoon*); or **where to?** (*to the movies*).

Exercise

Taking four of the subject-verb cores from any of the exercises you have done thus far in this section or inventing your own, write sentences whose subjects and verbs are modified. Use modifying phrases to add descriptive details and information about time, place, or direction. Circle and connect the subject and verb in each sentence.

Some Problems

Compound Modifiers

Sometimes you might want to add the idea that the person you are talking about has black hair but not want to use the phrase "with black hair" or put the idea into another sentence. In such a case, you can create a modifier *black-haired*. Notice, though, that two important changes must be made: If two words are involved in making the modifier, first, a hyphen (-) is inserted between them, and second, *-ed* is added or the past participle form of the verb is used.

Exercise

From the following ideas, create modifers and make up sentences in which you can use them. Add as many modifying words and phrases as you can.

Example: The old man had straggly hair.

The straggly-haired old man with the broken leg limped slowly past the store in the late afternoon.

1. The thin girl had dreamy eyes.
2. The fat dog had a bushy tail.
3. The old car had dents.

Circle the subject-verb core in each sentence.

Comparisons

Sometimes modifiers are used to express the idea that one object or action is different in some degree from another or from all others. In these cases you will need to use a special form of the word.

Example: John is brave<u>r</u> than his sister.

Joe is the brave<u>st</u> man in Squeduck.

If only one other person or object is involved, you need to add *er* to the modifier or add the word *more* or *less.*

Example: My hamburgers are *more* delicious than the ones at McDonald's.

My feet are *smaller* than Bill's.

If you want the modifier to express the idea that the person or object you are talking about is the top or the bottom in the quality you are discussing, use the words *most* or *least,* or the ending *-est.*

Example: The *smartest* boy in the class is Bill.

Jeanne is the *most* successful gymnast Hillcrest High School has ever had.

If the modifier ends in a *-y,* the *y* is usually changed to an *i* before the ending is added, as, for example, in the forms *happy, happier, happiest.*

Certain words have special forms for these comparisons, changing their form completely. Since these words are very common, you probably already are familiar with them.

When you are comparing in terms of how good or how bad something is, the proper forms are:

bad   good
worse   better
worst   best

If you want to say that one person's grades are not as good as anyone else's, you are comparing that person's grades with those of everyone else as though all the others were one unit. The proper form, therefore, is *worse.*

John's grades are *worse* than anyone else's.

If, however, you want to say John's grades are the lowest, you are comparing his grades with those of each member of the class. Then the correct word is *worst.*

John's grades are the *worst.*

With better and best, the same rule holds:

John's grades are *better* than anyone else's.

John's grades are the *best*.

If you wish to compare quantities, the forms are:

some, much	little, few
more	fewer, less
most	least

Note: If you cannot put the word *the* in front of the modifier, you need *worse* or *better*; if you need *the*, the proper form is *worst* or *best*.

Exercise

Write sentences in which you compare the following:

two oranges (juicy)
three cars (speed)
two basketball players (scorers)
five dancers (good and bad)

MORE WORK ON VERBS

Using -s As you learned in Chapter 4, one of the greatest difficulties is knowing when to put an -s at the end of a verb.

Simple Present Tense

Whenever you write in the present tense, you will need an -s on the main verb when the subject of the sentence is *he*, *she*, *it*, or words that can substitute for them.

Examples: Joe's radio *blares* all day long.

He *likes* to keep it very loud.

Joe *thinks* the music *sounds* better that way.

Exercise

Rewrite the following passage, substituting Al for I, and changing the verb as needed.

Most of my life I have been confused. Very little that I hear or see going on around me makes any sense. I don't always understand what people are doing. I take them on faith and play things by ear, which means that I have been let down a lot. But one of the few things that's never let me down is music — not musicians, not promoters, certainly not club owners, recording companies, critics or reviewers — music!

Special Verbs

The verb *to be* (that's the infinitive form of *is*, *are*, etc.) uses a form ending in *-s* for both the present and the past form when the subject is *he, she, it,* or words that substitute for them.

Examples: John *is* hoping to be a disk jockey.

He *was* working on the school radio station.

Interfering Words

Sometimes we have words between the subject and the verb that make it difficult to recognize the exact subject.

Examples: *One* of the boys *drives* to school.

All of the girls *wear* jeans.

The phrases *of the boys* and *of the girls* provide some necessary information about the subject of the sentences, but they are not the subjects. *One* is the subject of the first; *all* is the subject of the second.

Examples: The *grain* in the fields *looks* ripe.

A *group* of workers *is* fighting for a raise.

The *teacher*, together with her students, *stays* for the school play.

Exercise

Combine one of the words in group 1 below with the words in group 2 that fit, and then add as many words as you need to create a sentence in the present tense.

Group 1	Group 2
professor	along with his friends
snow	of the girls
mechanic	on the highways
one	of the singers
some	as well as the electricians

Test yourself: When you find the verb of the sentence, ask yourself who or what is doing the action. When it is one person, one place, one thing, or idea, be sure there is an -*s* on the verb if it is in the present tense.

Words That Cause Confusion

There are two groups that are difficult to work with.

Anyone, etc.

Anyone refers to just one person, as you can tell if you look at it carefully (see the *one?*). There are a number of words like *anyone* which always refer to just *one* person or *one* thing. When you use these words as the subject of the sentence in the present tense, you need an -*s* on the verb. Below is a list of those most frequently used:

anybody	somebody	neither
anyone	everybody	either
nobody	someone	everything
no one	everyone	nothing
none	each	something

Examples: *Everybody wants* to be a winner.

Everything costs too much.

Test yourself: Check to see if the word you are using as the subject of your sentence in the present tense ends in -*one*, -*body*, -*thing*. If it does, you know it will need an *s*. The other words that require the -*s* will have to be memorized.

Words Ending in -s

Some words end in -*s* even though they refer to one thing. Some of these words are

measles	economics
mathematics	news
mumps	physics

Despite the -*s*, these words are not plural forms; they need a verb with an -*s* in the present tense.

Examples: The *news is* good today, for a change.

Mathematics is my best subject.

Here and There

We often use the phrases *here is, here are, there is, there are* (also with *was* and *were*) to begin a sentence. *Here* and *there* are not, however, the subjects of these sentences. In such sentences, the subject comes after the verb.

Examples: Here *is* a beautiful *skateboard*.

There *are* five *reasons* why you should not quit school.

Test yourself: Find the verb and ask yourself *who* or *what is* (or *are*). If the answer to that question is *one* person, place, thing or idea, you need the *-s* form — *is*.

Exercise

Write five sentences using five different words from the list in the section *Anyone, etc.* Make sure these words are the subjects of the sentences and that your sentence is in the present. Choose your verb from the following list: *love, hate, want, try, give, take, play, run.*

Write five sentences using the words from the list in the section *Words Ending in -s* as the subjects. Be sure to use the present tense.

Write five sentences in the present tense that begin with *here* or *there*. Make the subject of three of them one person, place, thing, or idea.

MORE WORK ON VERBS

Irregular Verbs   While most English verbs form the past tense by adding *-ed*, a number of the most common ones do not follow this general rule. Instead they change their forms completely. Once you have memorized them, the only problem will be to make sure that you have used the appropriate forms. In the list of irregular verbs that follows this section, pp. 219–220, three forms of each verb are given. The first is used for the present tense, the second is used for the past, and the third is used with a form of *have* (*have, had, will have*).

Example: **drink drank drunk**

Tom and Bill *drink* a bottle of juice every day. (present)

Joe *drank* two bottles of grapefruit juice yesterday. (past)

Marie *had drunk* all the Kool Aid before her brothers came home. (form used with *have, had, will have* verbs)

Exercise
The following passage is written in the present tense. Rewrite it in the past tense; start by changing *every day* to *last week*. Use the simple past tense form (the one in the second column); do not use any combination forms. The first sentence will read, *Last week I got up at 5:30.*

Every day I *get* up at 5:30. I *throw* on my exercise suit and *tear* out of the house. I *see* the sun as it *rises* over the river while I *run* toward the park. I *begin* jogging right away because it *is* cold. When I *come* to the entrance, I *choose* my route for the day. I *break* into a fast trot. As I *fly* over the path, I *hear* the trucks rumblng down the avenue. In the beginning, I *sing* to myself or I *teach* myself irregular verb forms, but I *think* also how tired I *am* and I *steal* a short rest. Finally I *give* up and *go* back home. After I *take* my shower, I *sit* down at the table and *eat* a big bowl of Special K and *drink* a steaming cup of coffee.

Next, rewrite the passage again, this time changing *every day* to *frequently* and the verbs to the form with *have*. The rewritten version will begin: *Frequently I have gotten up* . . .
Below is a list of some of the most frequently used verbs with irregular forms.

I	II	III
am	was	been
begin	began	begun
break	broke	broken
bring	brought	brought
choose	chose	chosen
come	came	come
do	did	done
drink	drank	drunk
eat	ate	eaten
fly	flew	flown
freeze	froze	frozen
get	got	gotten
give	gave	given
go	went	gone

hear	heard	heard
know	knew	known
lend	lent	lent
ring	rang	rung
rise	rose	risen
run	ran	run
see	saw	seen
sing	sang	sung
sit	sat	sat
steal	stole	stolen
swim	swam	swum
take	took	taken
teach	taught	taught
tear	tore	torn
think	thought	thought
throw	threw	thrown
wear	wore	worn
write	wrote	written

MORE WORK ON SENTENCES

Verbals Sentence fragments often result when words are used that look like main verbs but aren't. These words end in either -ing or -ed. Since we associate both of these endings with verbs, we assume that we have written a complete sentence. Although these words name an action as verbs should, they do not tell the time period. For the main verb of a sentence we need both.

-ing Endings

When words like *playing, singing,* or *dancing* are used in a sentence, they must have a form of the verb *to be* (*is, are, was, were, will be,* etc.) to be complete.

Example: Mary *is singing* with a rock group.

If the sentence had been *Mary singing with a rock group,* we would not know whether the action is taking place now, took place in the past, or will happen in the future.

Exercise
Write six sentences using the words listed below as subjects. Begin two of them with the word *today,* two with *tomorrow,* and two with *yesterday.*

working   fighting   trying
studying   listening   dancing

More on -ing Endings

Sometimes words ending in -ing are used to add information to a sentence.

> *Example:* Mary walked out of the classroom, *leaving* her gloves on the chair.

It would be wrong to write: Mary walked out of the classroom. Leaving her gloves on the chair.

We would probably guess that the writer was still talking about Mary and that she left the gloves as she walked out of the classroom, but readers should not have to guess what a writer means to say.

Groups of words beginning with an -ing word may come before or after the sentence to which they belong.

> *Examples:* *Watching television,* Ronnie fell asleep.
>
> Ronnie fell asleep *watching television.*

Exercise
Read the following passage. Put in periods at the ends of sentences and capital letters for the first word of the next sentences.

Going into the supermarket Mary tried to remember what she was supposed to buy she stopped in front of the canned soups reading the labels she looked for a kind that was not too fattening she put down the can of Scotch Broth realizing that it contained 200 calories per serving she went to the soap display wondering which brand was best she finally decided to take the cheapest one she went to the checkout counter paying for her groceries with the last of her paycheck.

> *Test yourself:* When you see that you have used an -ing word in your writing, check to see if it gives the main action of the sentence. If it does, make sure there is a second verb with it — is, are, was, were, will be, etc.

If a sentence begins with an -ing verb, check to see if it is attached to a complete sentence.

-ed Endings

Since this ending is the usual one for regular verbs in the past tense, we automatically create a sentence when we put a noun in front of a verb with this ending.

Examples: John walked. Mary talked.

But this ending is also used for some words that can bring new ideas to our basic sentence.

Example: John, *tired from his long journey,* fell asleep at the kitchen table.

This same sentence could be written: John fell asleep at the kitchen table, tired from his long journey.

However, sometimes the writer will feel the sentence is finished at *table* and put a period there. Then we have: John fell asleep at the kitchen table. Tired from his long journey.

The readers must guess where the phrase *Tired . . .* belongs. Writers should always try to make their meaning as clear as possible.

Exercise

Use the following phrases in sentences of your own.
Make sure that you have a complete sentence before you add these phrases:

blinded by the spotlights
stretched out on the grass
dressed in her new embroidered
   shirt

annoyed at being disturbed
destroyed by drugs

Afterthoughts

Often when you are in the midst of writing a sentence, you get a few extra ideas and want to add them. Unless you intend to write a new sentence with a subject and verb, these added bits of information belong to the sentence you are working on.

Examples: When Joe hit a home run, everyone cheered wildly, *especially his girl friend, Karen.*

There are many sports you might want to try at the beach, *such as snorkeling, scuba diving, and surfing.*

It would be a mistake to write these sentences with a period before *especially* or *such as*, for the units that follow have no subject and no verb, and therefore are not sentences. Words that frequently introduce this kind of fragment are:

such as   also   including   except
especially   for instance   for example

Most fragments of this kind can be corrected by being attached to the preceding sentences. If you have used *for example* or *for instance*, however, you will have to create a whole new sentence with a subject and a verb.

Exercise
Write five sentences that include the words from the list.

Phrases

You wouldn't think of writing *Around the corner and into the station* as a sentence at the start of a paper, but sometimes when you get into your subject, you get carried away by the rhythm of your thinking. You might begin by writing *The man ran wildly down the street, dashing passed the startled ladies, bumping into the baby carriage. Around the corner and into the station.* You can see that the second unit clearly belongs to the first one; the period and the capital *A* should be removed.

Some of the phrases may even look like they have the main verb of a sentence in them.

Example: Jim wanted to be by himself. *Just to play the stereo in his room.*

The phrase *to play* does contain a verb, but in this form it can never be the main verb in a sentence. When there is a *to* in front of the verb, it needs other verbs (and also a subject) to form a complete sentence.

Test yourself: There is no substitute for checking every sentence you write until you have mastered these writing skills. It is dull and tedious, but it is necessary. Sometimes reading your essay from the last sentence to the first will make the mistakes stand out more clearly.

Joining Words As you learned in Chapter 7, words like *because, after, while, although,* etc., are used to join two ideas
together. If only one of the ideas is given in the sentence, the
meaning is unclear and the reader is confused. When the joining
word comes between the two ideas, you can spot it fairly easily,
and correct it.

> *Example:* **(Wrong)** Bill kept his eyes on the floor. Because
> he did not want the teacher to call on
> him.
>
> **(Correct)** Bill kept his eyes on the floor because
> he did not want the teacher to call on
> him.

The *because* should join the two ideas, so you can correct the sentence simply by removing the period and the capital *B*.

The problem, unfortunately, is not always that simple, for the
joining word is often put at the beginning of the sentence, and
then it may be difficult to remember which sentence it belongs to.
You should not stop beginning sentences with these words; in
fact, it is an important way to add variety to your sentences. But it
does put an added burden on you, and you must check each sentence carefully.

Exercise

Complete the following sentences. As you can see, each
joining word and idea has been used twice, once to begin the
sentence and then as the ending:

1. **a.** Because I am always late for class, _____.
   b. _____ because I am always late for class.
2. **a.** While my cousin Millie was getting dressed, _____.
   b. _____ while my cousin Millie was getting dressed.
3. **a.** After I finish studying for my math test, _____.
   b. _____, after I finish studying for my math test.
4. **a.** Although the work at Kraus' hardware store is not hard,
   _____.
   b. _____ although the work at Kraus' hardware store is not
   hard.
5. **a.** Unless Mary quits teasing me, _____.
   b. _____ unless Mary quits teasing me.

Test yourself: When checking your own writing, you will have
to read both the sentence that comes *before* the

joining word and the sentence that comes after it in order to determine which one it belongs to.

Who, Which, That Another group of connecting words that can cause fragments are *who, whom, whose, which,* and *that.* These words operate differently from others, for they perform a triple function. In the first place, they act as pronouns, taking the place of the nouns to which they refer. The forms of *who* are used for people; *which* is used for places and things; and *that* may be used for all.

> *Example:* The boy *who* sang the tenor solo in the church choir is also the lead singer for the Ginger Peachy Rock group.

In the above sentence, *who* substitutes for *boy.* At the same time, it is the subject of the verb *sang. Who* has still a third job in the sentence: It is the connecting word as well. It links together the ideas first, that the boy sang in the church choir and second, that he is the lead singer of a rock group. Like all linking words, *who, which,* and *that* are signals to your readers that there will be two ideas in the sentence. Whenever you use one of these words in your sentence, you must check to see that you have included two subject-verb cores, each expressing an idea.

You need commas to separate the part of the sentence that begins with *who, which,* or *that* if it interrupts the main thought of the sentence. If it is a necessary part of the main idea, you do not need any commas.

Combine the two sentences in each of the following units into one sentence by using *who, which,* or *that.*

> *Example:* Dr. Feelgood has just written a new book. He is a leading expert on nutrition.
>
> Dr. Feelgood, *who is a leading expert on nutrition, has just written a new book.* OR
>
> Dr. Feelgood, *who has just written a new book, is a leading expert on nutrition.*

1. The new book is a bestseller.
   It is entitled *Eat Less, Gain More: A Guide to Eating Efficiency.*
2. Dr. Feelgood believes that Canadians waste time and energy unnecessarily because of their poor eating habits. Canadians spend over three hours a day eating.

3. According to Dr. Feelgood, fruits and vegetables are a waste because they supply so few calories. Fruits and vegetables take a great deal of time to consume.
4. A fresh pear takes at least ten minutes to eat.
A fresh pear supplies only 265 kJ.
5. On the other hand, a chocolate donut supplies 1150 kJ.
A chocolate donut can be eaten in seven minutes.
6. Dr. Feelgood claims we should apply assembly-line techniques to all our meals and snacks.
Assembly-line techniques are known around the world for their efficiency.
7. Because of this efficiency we will have more free time for important activities like sleeping.
This efficiency will save hours every day.
8. Dr. Feelgood says, "We may be fat, but we'll be efficient."
Dr. Feelgood has a mass of 170 kg.

MORE WORK ON SENTENCES

Run-On   Every sentence needs one subject-verb core, but one is enough. If you omit the period between two complete sentences, or if you put in a comma where a stronger separation is needed, you will create confusion in your reader's mind.

Omitted Linking Words

Often when you write you think of a connection between two ideas, but by the time you transfer your thoughts to paper, you leave out the word that links those ideas. For instance, you might write: *Gladys gave a loud cheer, she had passed Chemistry 101.* What you probably were thinking was that Gladys gave the cheer *because* she had passed Chemistry 101. You may have left the linking word out on the theory that your readers would automatically know what the connection was, but in this example and in many others like it, your readers could have thought of several other possibilities. They might, for instance, have substituted *when, since, after,* or *for.* You need to make your exact meaning clear. Sometimes you may put a comma between *cheer* and *she,* but a comma cannot be used to separate two complete thoughts.

The run-ons that result from this kind of omission can be corrected by putting a period at the end of the first thought and starting the next word with a capital letter. But the result in most cases would be two choppy sentences. It is far better to use the linking word that not only fixes the error but conveys your meaning, as well.

Note: In many run-ons caused by the omission of a linking word, you will find a *he, she, it, they, we, you, this, that,* or *I* in the middle of the sentence. Any sentence in which one of these words appears in the middle should be checked carefully. Read it out loud if necessary. Count the subject-verb cores, and if there is more than one, make sure there is a linking word.

Exercise

In the following passage, all end punctuation has been omitted. Supply any connecting words you think are needed and all necessary periods. Do not insert any commas; all the necessary ones have been supplied.

The whole class was excited Janet was thrilled she got an A on her essay Julio was relieved he had expected to fail, but had managed to get a C− Maria was happy, too, she read the teacher's comment praising her organization Willard smiled at the note in the margin the teacher had asked who Fleetwood Mac was everyone felt better Composition class wasn't as bad as they had expected.

Confusion Over Linking Words

Certain words appear to be linking words, but, although they are important ways of connecting ideas, they are not words that can join sentences. The following words fall into this category:

now	then
therefore	however
moreover	consequently

If, by mistake, you have used these words to link sentences, you can correct your error either by putting in a period before the word and starting a new sentence with a capital letter, or you may use a semicolon before the word. **Note:** You may need a comma following each of these words.

Example: John read the textbook three times, studied his class notes for 20 hours and made up an outline of three answers to possible essay-exam questions; consequently, he received an A+ on his history exam.

Exercise

Write a second sentence to go with each of the following sentences. Use the words in parentheses as the first word of your sentence.

1. The first thing that went wrong this morning was that I turned off the alarm clock in my sleep.
   (Then) ————

2. When I took the milk out of the refrigerator the bottom fell out of the container.
   (Therefore) ————

3. While I was crying over the spilt milk, my dog walked through the kitchen, getting each paw thoroughly soaked.
   (However) ————

4. I went out to start the car, but the battery was dead.
   (Consequently) ————

5. I had to wait 45 minutes for the bus in the freezing cold.
   (Now) ————

MORE WORK ON PUNCTUA-TION

Commas   Of all the marks of punctuation, the comma seems to cause the most confusion to beginning writers. For the most part, commas indicate a short pause inside a sentence. But not all pauses require a comma, and many beginning writers put commas in places where they are not only unnecessary but wrong. If you thoroughly learn the five situations in which a comma must be used and then use a comma only in those places, you may avoid some serious errors.

Dates, Addresses, Opening and Closing of Letters, Numbers

A comma is necessary between name of the day and month, as well as between the date and the year.

A comma is necessary between the street address and name of city, as well as between city and state.

A comma is necessary after the opening greeting and after the closing of a letter.

Dear Mr. Smith,
   On Monday, January 27, 1978, I took the civil service examination for pothole inspector at your headquarters at 179

Wrattling Road, Bumpton, Alberta. 4 280 other men and
women also took the exam, but no one has yet been hired.
When will the results be published?

Yours truly,

B. Roken Axelrod

Direct Quotations

A comma is necessary to set direct quotations off from
the rest of a sentence.

"Pet cobras are fun," said Maizie, "especially when
they are as cute and cuddly as my Spot."

Commas before *and, but, for, so,* and *or* when these words
connect two fairly long complete thoughts

Before you use a comma in this situation, be sure there is a
connecting word (*and, but,* etc.). *The comma cannot substitute for
the connecting word.*

Many people think that cobras do not make good pets,
but they should read Dr. Venom's book *Owning Cobras for
Fun and Profit.*

Separating items in a series

When you have several items together in a sentence, you need
commas to separate them.

Cobras like a warm place to sleep, a juicy rat to eat, and
someone to love.
Maizie's cobra has black, white, and brown spectacle-
shaped marks on his hood.
Spot raises his soft, limpid, beady eyes whenever Maizie
whistles.

Commas are needed to separate interrupters

When you add words that interrupt the flow of the sentence,
separate them from the rest of the sentence with commas.

Spot, who loves to warm himself on the windowsill,
slithers to the door when Maizie comes home.
If she is late, however, he sulks in the corner.

Be sure that the words you set off actually interrupt the sentence and are not necessary to the meaning.

The snake that bit Josephina was not Spot.

Since the words *that bit Josephina* are necessary to the meaning you do not need commas.

Commas are needed after introductory material

When you supply information before the main part of the sentence you need to separate it with a comma.

When Spot learned that he was accused of biting Josephina, he pouted for three days.
Looking soulfully at the ceiling, he ignored all of Maizie's efforts to cheer him up.
Finally, he consented to leave his corner when Maizie offered him a plump field mouse.

If you begin with only a short phrase you do not need a comma.

In the morning Spot was his usual cheerful self.

Test yourself: Put in all necessary commas:

117 East Asp Street
Slippery Rock, Alberta

May 10 1979

Dear Dr. Venom

After reading your book *Cobras for Fun and Profit* I want to thank you for adding so much to my pleasure in life. Maizie Turner who lent me your book has told me about your plans to write a sequel *Quick Cures for Snakebite.* Such a book would be interesting useful and definitely an important addition to all snake-lovers' libraries. I had often wanted to own my own snake but until I read your book I had little understanding of how exciting a hobby it could be. Now however I have my own little Mathilda to cheer my lonely hours. As I said to Maizie just the other day "Snakes bring peace and quiet into a home. Not one of those sales people who always used to annoy me have I seen since Mathilda has come to live with me."

Please Dr. Venom send me a copy of your new book as soon as it is published.

Sincerely yours

MORE WORK ON CAPITALS

Names and Sentences The use of capital letters varies from country to country and from one age to another. Spanish- and French-speaking countries use it much less frequently than English-speaking countries, but at the same time its use in English-speaking countries has declined in the last 200 years.

The general rule is to use a capital letter for:

1. The name of a particular person, place, or thing
2. The first word of a sentence

Capitals and Names

1. A capital is used when a word names a particular person, place, or thing. If there is a title with a person's name, it should also be capitalized.

Examples: Ms. Monica Aldrich, Senator Daniel Webster, Rear Admiral Farragut, General Stephen Decatur, Nikki Giovanni, Hepzibah Pyncheon, Mother Jones, France, Nigeria, Pikes Peak, Red River, Wok-A-Do Restaurant, the Golden Gate Bridge, Sears Tower, Maple Street.

2. Certain words are *always capitalized:* Names of cities, countries, languages, months of the year, days of the week, holidays, sacred names, the word *I* (when writing about oneself).

Examples: On Monday, September 6, 1978, while living in Cairo, Egypt, I began an intensive study of the Koran in the original Arabic.

Even when you are using words derived from these names, you need the capital letter.

Example: Every Canadian should know some French.

3. If a word is used in a general sense, it is not capitalized.

Words like *country, lawyer, ocean, southern hemisphere, father* are not capitalized except when they are part of a particular name.

Special Note: When the word *river* is part of the name of a particular river, the r is capitalized; if the word *river* is used to refer to an unspecified body of water, the r is not capitalized. In the examples above, the words *mother, peak, river, restaurant, golden, gate, bridge, tower, maple,* and *street* are all capitalized because they appear as parts of particular names; otherwise they would not be.

4. Other kinds of names that need capitals are names of business organizations, religious and political groups, associations, unions, and clubs. Names of *particular* groups are capitalized.

> *Example:* General Motors Corporation has signed a special contract with the United Auto Workers Union to cover the assembly plant in Oshawa, Ontario.

Names of commercial products are capitalized.

> *Example:* On April Fool's Day, my little sister covered a cake with whipped Crest toothpaste instead of RediWhip. We took one taste and rushed to the bathroom to wash our mouths out with Listerine.

Names of titles of books, magazines, movies, television shows, newspapers, articles, stories, songs, and record albums also use capitals for the main words. You do not need to capitalize *of, an, the* unless they are the first word.

> *Examples:* Gone with the Wind, Newsweek, The Sting, etc.

Capitals to Start Sentences

1. The first letter of the first word of a sentence must be a capital letter.

> *Example:* My lawyer assured me I would win my case if I could find one witness who would say he saw me in the bar that night.

2. The first word of a sentence in a direct quotation is capitalized.

> *Example:* Maggie said, "Arthur is too gentle to be a boxer."

Even when the words quoted do not make a complete sentence, the first letter is still capitalized.

> *Example:* Joe answered, "Why not?"

But if the sentence of the direct quotation is interrupted by naming the speaker, you do not need to use a capital for the continuation of the quote.

Example: "If Arthur would only get mad," answered Joe, "he'd knock out three men with one punch."

Exercise

Provide capitals as needed in the following passage.

When i registered at orange county community college this fall i found it was a lot different from my old high school. i ran into a number of serious problems. i needed to take english 015, a course in writing, but by the time i got up to the head of the line, all the sections that fit into my schedule were closed. i also had to take a mathematics course, and i had signed up for math 105, section 4. if i changed to section 3, i could get a space in the english 015 course, so i rushed over to the math registration section. the line there was long, too, and the students kept crowding closer and closer together. the guy in back of me had had a salami sandwich for lunch and i wished i had a bottle of scope or some dentyne chewing gum to give him before his breath knocked me out. i wanted to take a course in the history of south america because i've always been interested in the inca influence on the spanish settlers, but the only course available was history 403 which is restricted to juniors and seniors. finally i decided to sign up for a course in comparative religion in which the ideas of christians, jews, moslems, and hindus are discussed.

LANGUAGE PROBLEMS

The Letter S The letter s serves so many different functions in English that it is quite easy to mix up the rules and apply them incorrectly. When this happens, mistakes are made. To prevent this, here is a list of all the special uses of the letter s.

1. S is used to form most plural nouns

When you want to refer to more than one of a person, place or thing, you usually add an s to the noun.

boy	boys	dream	dreams
girl	girls	house	houses
job	jobs	school	schools
desk	desks		

This *s* is added directly to the word; *you do not need an apostrophe* ('). In fact, if you do use an apostrophe, you are making an error that will confuse your reader.

For some words, the *s* sound cannot be pronounced unless an *e* is added as well (-*es*).

box   boxes
match   matches

For some words, more elaborate changes have to be made before the *s* is added.

leaf   leaves
knife   knives
wife   wives

2. S is used on present tense verbs when the subject of the sentence is *he, she, it,* or a word that can substitute for them.

Joe works at Rite-Aid Drug Store.
Mary sings at the Black Cat Club.

The *s* is the proper ending for this use of the verb. If it is omitted, the verb will not be in the form that agrees with its subject.

Many students think of the *s* only as a letter for forming plurals. When they see that they have only one person, place, or thing for the subject of their sentences, they think no *s* is needed for the rest of the sentence.

Try to remember that there is one rule for *s* on nouns and a different rule for *s* on verbs.

3. S is the last letter of the possessive pronouns *its, yours, ours,* and *theirs.*

The tree lost *its* leaves.
This book is *ours,* that one is *theirs,* and the one on the table is *yours.*

These words are properly spelled with an *s* as their last letter. It is wrong and confusing to use an apostrophe.

4. S is used to show ownership with nouns.

When you want to show ownership with a noun, you do so by adding '*s.*

Bill has a pen — Bill's pen
Mary has a new dress — Mary's new dress

Joe has interesting ideas — Joe's interesting ideas
The book has pages — The book's pages

If the apostrophe is omitted, your reader will be momentarily confused and may think you are writing a plural. *Bills pen* suggests that there is more than one man named Bill. *The books pages* suggests that there is more than one book. Unless your readers mentally supply the apostrophe for you, your words will not make sense to them.

Remember, however, that you do not add an apostrophe for *its, yours, ours, theirs* when you are indicating ownership.

Note: There is a special problem that arises when the word you are using ends in s. In that case, the apostrophe goes after the s. This situation most often occurs when you are writing about more than one person, place, or thing, that is, using plurals.

The three boys' book bags were thrown down in the hallway.

5. 'S is used as a short form of *is* or *has.*

Instead of writing *it is,* you may often write *it's.* (For *It is time to go,* you may often write *It's time to go.* The 's stands for the omitted *i* in *is.*)

The apostrophe is important to indicate that a letter has been left out. If you omit the apostrophe in the sentence and write *Its time to go,* your readers may think that the *its* indicates ownership and will not understand your sentence until they add an apostrophe for themselves.

(Acknowledgments continued)

Six   Pages 73–74 Mystery from *School Primer No. 4 Zephyros.* Assembled by Ron Jones. Game by Aaron Hellman.
Pages 78–82 "August Heat" from *The Beast with Five Fingers* by William Fryer Harvey. Copyright 1947 by E. P. Dutton. Reprinted by permission of the publishers, E. P. Dutton & Co., Inc. and J. M. Dent & Sons Ltd.

Seven   Pages 94–98 "The Pedestrian" by Ray Bradbury, © 1964 by Ray Bradbury. Reprinted by permission of Harold Matson Company, Inc.

Eight   Pages 107–110 "After You, My Dear Alphonse" from *The Lottery* by Shirley Jackson, Copyright 1948, 1949 by Sirley Jackson, renewed © 1976 by Laurence Hyman, Barry Hyman, Mrs. Sarah Webster, and Mrs. Joanne Schnurer. Reprinted with the permission of Farrar, Straus & Giroux, Inc.

Nine   Pages 118–119 "Divorce — Teenage Style" from Donald Mills, *Generating the Paragraph and Short Essay,* © 1970. Reprinted by permission of Prentice-Hall, Inc., Englewood Cliffs, N.J.
Pages 121–122 James Tuite, "The Sounds of the City," *The New York Times,* August 6, 1966 © 1966 by The New York Times Company. Reprinted by permission.

Ten   Page 134 From *Roots* by Alex Haley. Copyright © 1976 by Alex Haley. Used by permission of Doubleday & Company, Inc.
Page 135 © 1957 by Mary McCarthy. Excerpted from "Ask Me No Questions" in *Memories of a Catholic Girlhood by Mary McCarthy* by permission of Harcourt Brace Jovanovich, Inc. First published in *The New Yorker.*
Pages 138–141 "On the Way to Being Real," from *Person to Person: The Problems of Being Human* by Carl Rogers and Barry Stevens. Reprinted by permission of Real People Press, Box F, Moab, Utah 84532
Page 141 "Nikki-Rosa" from *Black Feeling, Black Talk, Black Judgment* by Nikki Giovanni. Copyright © 1968, 1970 by Nikki Giovanni. By permission of William Morrow & Company, Inc.
Page 142 "Unwanted," from *Stand Up, Friend, with Me* by Edward Field. Copyright © 1963 by Edward Field. Reprinted by permission of Grove Press, Inc.
Pages 142–143 "Second Nature" by Diana Chang, from *New York Quarterly,* Spring 1972, No. 11. Reprinted by permission.
Pages 143–144 "The Chance," which originally appeared in *Ararat* (Summer 1968), from *The Northern Wall* (Northeastern University Press), copyright © 1969 by Harold Bond. Reprinted by permission.
Pages 144–145 "Aztec Angel" by Omar Salinas from *Crazy Gypsy* (Fresno, California: Origenes Publications, 1970). Reprinted by permission of the poet.

Twelve   Pages 164–171 "Wet Saturday," from *Fancies and Goodnights.* Copyright 1940, renewed © 1968 by John Collier. Reprinted by permission of Harold Matson Company, Inc.

Thirteen   Pages 185–186 "Beating Writer's Block," reprinted by permission from *Time,* The Weekly Newsmagazine (October 31, 1977); copyright Time Inc. 1977.
Pages 187–188 From Ernest Hemingway, "When You Camp Out, Do It Right," *Toronto Star Weekly,* June 26, 1920, p. 17. Reprinted by permission of Alfred Rice, for the Estate of Ernest Hemingway; © Ernest Hemingway.

Fourteen   Pages 195–196 Copyright 1940 by James Thurber, © 1968 by Helen Thurber. From *Fables for Our Time,* published by Harper & Row. Originally published in The New Yorker.
Art
Pages 23 and 86–89. Photos from Stock, Boston, by the following: page 23, Frank Siteman; page 86, Stephen J. Potter; page 87 top, Charles Gatewood; bottom, Ira Kirschenbaum; page 88 top, Donald Dietz; bottom, Frank Siteman; page 89 top, Jack Prelutsky; bottom, Patricia Hollander Gross.
Page 130 Collage by Eddie Lopez.
Page 131 Collage by Tonia Noell-Roberts.
Page 200 Photo from Ontario Archives; page 201 Photo from *The Toronto Star.*